1950

New Library of Pastoral Care
GENERAL EDITOR: DEREK BLOWS

Derek Blows is the Director of the Westminster Pastoral
Foundation and a psychotherapist at University College
Hospital. He is also an honorary canon of Southwark
Cathedral.

City of God?

Titles in this series include:

New Library of Pastoral Care
GENERAL EDITOR: DEREK BLOWS

———

CITY OF GOD?

Pastoral Care in the Inner City

———

Nicholas Bradbury

First published in Great Britain 1989
SPCK
Holy Trinity Church
Marylebone Road
London NW1 4DU

British Library Cataloguing in Publication Data

Bradbury, Nicholas
    City of God? : pastoral care in the inner
    city.
    1. Christian church. Pastoral work
    I. Title
    253

    ISBN 0-281-04351-5

Filmset by Pioneer, Perthshire
Printed and bound in Great Britain by
Courier International Ltd, Tiptree, Essex

Contents

Foreword

The *New Library of Pastoral Care* has been planned to meet the needs of those people concerned with pastoral care, whether clergy or lay, who seek to improve their knowledge and skills in this field. Equally, it is hoped that it may prove useful to those secular helpers who may wish to understand the role of the pastor.

Pastoral care in every age has drawn from contemporary secular knowledge to inform its understanding of man and his various needs and of the ways in which these needs might be met. Today it is perhaps the secular helping professions of social work, counselling and psychotherapy, and community development which have particular contributions to make to the pastor in his work. Such knowledge does not stand still, and a pastor would have a struggle to keep up with the endless tide of new developments which pour out from these and other disciplines, and to sort out which ideas and practices might be relevant to his particular pastoral needs. Among present-day ideas, for instance, of particular value might be an understanding of the social context of the pastoral task, the dynamics of the helping relationship, the attitudes and skills as well as factual knowledge which might make for effective pastoral intervention and, perhaps most significant of all, the study of particular cases, whether through verbatim reports of interviews or general case presentation. The discovery of ways of learning from what one is doing is becoming increasingly important.

There is always a danger that a pastor who drinks deeply at the well of a secular discipline may lose his grasp of his own pastoral identity and become 'just another' social worker or counsellor. It in no way detracts from the value of these professions to assert that the role and task of the pastor are quite unique among the helping professions and deserve to be clarified and strengthened rather than weakened. The theological commitment of the pastor and the appropriate use of his role will be a recurrent theme of the series. At the same time the pastor cannot afford to work in a vacuum. He needs to be able to communicate and co-operate with those helpers in other disciplines whose work may overlap, without loss of his own unique role. This in turn will mean being able to communicate with them through some understanding of their concepts and language.

Finally, there is a rich variety of styles and approaches in pastoral work within the various religious traditions. No attempt will be made to secure a uniform approach. The Library will contain the variety, and even perhaps occasional eccentricity, which such a title suggests. Some books will be more specifically theological and others more concerned with particular areas of need or practice. It is hoped that all of them will have a usefulness that will reach right across the boundaries of religious denomination.

DEREK BLOWS
Series Editor

Acknowledgements

The congregations of the Elephant Group of Churches at the Elephant and Castle in South London and Holy Trinity, Tottenham in North London provided most of the experience which has made this book possible. John Austin Baker (my tutor), Keith Pound (my first incumbent), Henley James, Pamela Maggs, Ken Sheekey and Gloria Wright (staff colleagues in Tottenham) and Gordon Mursell (steadfast friend and fellow traveller) have greatly helped me in my attempt to relate experience and theology. Jan McGregor must be thanked for what she has taught me and for permitting me to include a description of the Holy Trinity, Tottenham Pastoral Visiting Scheme as Chapter Twelve since we created the training programme entirely together. I am also particularly indebted to the staff and students of Salisbury and Wells Theological College; the staff and members of the Tavistock Institute's Consultation course (1986—88); my parents; Paul Bates; Peter Neary; Léonce and Odile Mottin; Peter Bellamy; Terry Roberts; John Barrett; Beau Stevenson; Cathy, Olivia and Huw; and to Stephen Slade for valuable advice in the preparation of the final manuscript. I am also grateful to Viv Dench, Sally Mathieson and Helen Watson for their typing.

All names in illustrations from the parishes have been changed and the accounts of St Aloysius and All Incense, St Paul and the Holy Table, St Jumbo's, the Parish Church, St Luke's Stressborough and All Saints, Easterhope, though drawn from life, are fictional. I feel I must acknowledge the impact on me of John Hull's *What Prevents Christian Adults from Learning?* (SCM 1985), prescribed reading for all pastors, and which helped me particularly in my preparation of Chapter Five. James D. Anderson and Ezra Earl Jones' book, *The Management of Ministry* (Harper & Row 1978) was similarly helpful for Chapter Eight. Many other books were influential and these are mentioned in the notes. My greatest debt in preparing this book is to the people of the Elephant and Castle (1973−6) and Tottenham (1979−85) and especially, amongst those who have died, to Beattie Cox, James Davis, Wendy Farkas, Stephen Faulkner and Charlie Tomkins, all of whom, in very different ways, showed indelible signs of the glory of God.

NICHOLAS BRADBURY
Michaelmas Day 1988

Introduction

Climb to the top of the Nat West tower in London, the tallest building in the City. On a clear day you can see all London and far south beyond Crystal Palace to the North Downs. You can watch jet planes make their gradual descent from Kent to Heathrow, while to the north you can see to Hampstead Heath and Alexandra Palace.

It is easy to feel overwhelmed by the immensity of a big city and it can be liberating to see that even London comes to an end. There in the distance is Epping Forest to prove it.

For the housebound widow, elderly and alone, looking out from the eighth floor of her tower block, there may never be the relief of such a liberating vantage point. From her balcony she may see only a vandalized parking lot full of burnt out cars, broken glass, dumped Tesco's trolleys and racist graffiti. This woman and millions of other people, find their lives crippled by the inner city environment in which they have to live: *Here w? go!! who creates the Tony blocks?*

> The inner city is the social antipodes of middle-class Britain, a universe apart, an alien world devoid of almost every feature of an ideal environment. It is the place where all our social ills come together, the place where all our sins are paid for ... (It) is a microcosm of deprivation, of economic decline and of social disintegration. . . . a symbol and summation of the dark side of a whole society.[1]

In July 1983 the Archbishop of Canterbury's Commission on Urban Priority Areas was appointed to see how both Church and Nation might address themselves to this situation. Their report, *Faith in the City*,[2] was published two years later in a welter of political controversy. It recommends solutions which would necessitate far-reaching changes in our social, economic and ecclesiastical institutions. But though rooted in theology

1

and pastoral concern it does not seek to offer a detailed strategy for the development of parish pastoral care. For the pastor and congregation of an inner city parish, however, it is of the utmost importance that they should work out such a strategy for themselves. The aim of this book is to help in this task. In it I have tried to draw on both theology and the human sciences to show how an inner city congregation can become a lively and effective agent of pastoral care. Part One provides an overview of the pastoral problems posed for the churches by the inner city. It concludes with a sketch of the Church of England in the inner city.

In Part Two the pastoral resources available to inner city congregations are more fully discussed and the necessary conditions for their development laid out.

Part Three takes up specific subjects of central importance to the implementation of parish pastoral care in practice.

One major and recurring theme of the book will be corporateness: the way in which a congregation belongs together as a worshipping, learning, healing and serving community. Ministerial leadership is of course essential in the enabling of such corporateness. But the tasks of parish pastoral care, for clear theological and practical reasons, are the responsibility of the congregation as a whole.

In *Faith in the City* the term 'Urban Priority Area' is used to include inner city districts and other areas of social deprivation many of which are to be found in the *outer* areas of large cities. In this book the term 'inner city' is used synonymously with 'urban priority area'. It is similarly intended to refer both to inner and outer estates, and so to a recognizable kind of human environment rather than to a specific geographical location.

The term *pastor* here refers to anyone acting in some accredited role as a pastor, whether clerical or lay, professional or voluntary.

Notes

1. P. Harrison, *Inside the Inner City,* Penguin 1983, p. 21.
2. The Report of the Archbishop of Canterbury's Commission on Urban Priority Areas, *Faith in the City,* Church House Publishing 1985.

PART ONE

The Predicament of the Inner City

ONE

The External Environment

'Hear, Lord, and act! For your own sake, my God do not
delay, because they bear your name, this is your city, this
is your people.'

Daniel 9.19

Housing and landscape

All analyses of the inner city agree that it is not one or other
particular feature of the environment which dehumanizes but
the combination and interaction of multiple problems. This
point is particularly important in an assessment of inner city
housing. It is common for suburban or rural residents visiting
the inner city for the first time honestly to feel, as they are
shown round a new estate, that the flats seem rather pleasant.
Someone once remarked to me that the red brick Rockingham
Estate, notorious in Southwark, reminded them of the
Dolphin Square luxury flats in Pimlico. I was not surprised.
For if flats are newly painted and have some geraniums in
their window-boxes, and if the recently completed Council
landscaping is as yet unvandalized, inner city blocks of flats
can appear pleasant enough. And since middle-class people
import their own assumptions about life-style which do not
take into account the constraints of inner city life, there is a
natural tendency to resist drawing appropriate conclusions.
'It must be nice not to have to worry about a garden.' 'Some
people like living high up—New York apartments are more
expensive on the top floors.' 'It's probably very neighbourly.'
'If they leave London for a weekend they're always glad to get
back, you know.'

These comments, and many like them, carry a sufficient
grain of truth for their speakers often to resist facing the
plain fact that the quality of inner city housing is generally
lamentable. It represents in solid brick, steel, concrete, glass,

5

[handwritten margin note: The Macmillan are now 300,000 houses a year!]

and tarmac the physical proof of our society's apparently
permanent refusal to build an urban environment appropriate
to the human needs of its poorer members. Lloyd George
wanted homes fit for heroes to live in after the First World
War. They were not built then, and despite ambitious
programmes of slum clearance and high rise developments in
the intervening seventy years our housing problems remain
intractable. In 1981 the Audit Commission estimated that in
England alone there were over a million dwellings unfit for
human habitation. Between 1979 and 1986 public spending
on housing fell in real terms by almost two thirds. The Audit
Commission now estimates that £30—£40 bn would be
needed to put our public and private housing stock into a
reasonable state of repair. *Faith in the City*'s stand on housing
is simple and clear. The report sees housing as a major issue.
It states: 'Living conditions are such a basic necessity that
they affect well-being in every aspect of life.'[1] It draws
attention to the feelings shared by so many people living in
the urban priority areas of powerlessness, of not being in
control of their own lives, of being devalued. It sees that these
feelings are made worse by 'the stigma which attaches to
certain people because of where they live'. It lays bare
particular injustices in housing as they apply to single people,
women and black people, and draws this conclusion: 'We
have examined the structure of housing in the urban priority
areas (UPAs), looking particularly at how it meets the needs
of the poorer members of our society, and have found it
totally inadequate. It is clear to us that the present housing
situation of the UPAs is quite unacceptable.'[2]

There is widespread evidence to support such a conclusion.
Lord Scarman's Report on the Brixton disorders of 1981[3] has
scathing remarks to make about the housing conditions of
Lambeth and the social significance of this. It is strongly
reinforced by the Report of the Inquiry into British Housing,
chaired by the Duke of Edinburgh (1985). The squalid
housing conditions of one typical urban priority area,
Hackney, are graphically and horrifically described by Paul
Harrison in his book *Inside the Inner City*. The issues and
their challenge are continually restated by the Child Poverty
Action Group[4] and the National Federation of Housing
Associations.[5]

To put this sociological data into a personal perspective, I invite you to consider your response to this question: What type of housing would you regard as the ideal for you and your family? I have asked various parish groups this question and given them ten minutes to draw up a list. If yours is a typical middle-class English family your list is unlikely to differ much from the following response of a Lent group in Dorset, which is about average. The features which were important to them were

— privacy;
— good views and a setting of natural beauty;
— peaceful surroundings;
— safe play space for children;
— friendly neighbours;
— enough bedrooms to entertain guests overnight;
— a spacious kitchen;
— two bathrooms, if possible.

From a UPA perspective this list is striking for what it omits. It assumes that the accommodation will be dry, and that it can be heated, that the fabric is not in a state of decay and that it is not infested with vermin. In the inner city however these things cannot be taken for granted. 37,648 households were disconnected by London Electricity in 1980. The Audit Commission's estimate of £40 bn for repairs to the housing stock is for putting right *fundamental* problems of structural safety, damp, hopelessly inadequate sound insulation (in my brand new high rise Southwark council flat as a curate I could easily hear my neighbour's gentle breathing when he was asleep), excessive heat loss and a lack of one or more basic amenities.

According to Harrison:

In 1979—80 one in five dwellings in Hackney was unfit for human habitation. Another twenty-two per cent of dwellings were in substantial disrepair. In material terms that means sodden basements, leaking roofs, draughty windows, perpetually peeling paper and crumbling plaster; in human terms: damp, cold, rheumatism, respiratory diseases and depression.[6]

In fact, inner city housing often provides a reality which contrasts starkly with the middle class ideal:

- 'nothing the neighbours don't know' rather than privacy;
- smelly, graffiti-covered stair-wells, ugly surroundings and unrelenting concrete and tarmac to look at;
- rubbish and dirt all around;
- the ceaseless noise of traffic, ghetto-blasters and screaming children;
- danger for children;
- anonymous neighbours;
- cramped accommodation with no spare room.

Such conditions amply justify the accusing question sprayed over the base of a tower block in Southwark, 'Homes or filing cabinets?'.

Unemployment

Unemployment in Britain's Development Areas stood, in June 1988, at 15.5%. Among the ethnic minorities the figure was estimated to be 31%. The number of school leavers who by September 1987 had yet to find a job was 36,000. Of all the unemployed the percentage of those who had been without work for more than one year was 41%: for more than three years, 20%.[7]

These figures speak for themselves when you stop thinking in statistics and think rather of what it must feel like to have left school more than a year ago, have still not found a job, and see no prospect of one.

In his report on the Brixton disorders Lord Scarman puts it like this:

Unemployment remains an evil that touches all of the community. There can be no doubt that it was a major factor in the complex pattern of conditions which lies at the root of the disorders in Brixton and elsewhere. In a materialistic society, the relative deprivation it entails is keenly felt, and idleness gives time for resentment and envy to grow. When there is added the natural aggression of youth and with the media ever present to relay examples of violence, there arises a devastating and dangerous combination of factors tending to unrest and disorder.[8]

Lord Scarman's perspective is that of a judge. Archbishop William Temple saw it somewhat differently. In the autumn of 1934 he wrote to *The Times* of his concern for the unemployed:

> The gravest evil and bitterest injury of their state is not the animal grievance of hunger or discomfort, nor even the mental grievance of vacuity and boredom; it is the spiritual grievance of being allowed no opportunity of contributing to the general life and welfare of the community. All efforts for their assistance should therefore look towards the provision of that opportunity.

The extent of our failure to heed Temple's words is reflected in the letter Professor Ralf Dahrendorf wrote to *The Times* after the soccer riots on the terraces in Brussels by British fans in May 1985. He suggests that in some places soccer has become an 'under-class' game, and associates its hooliganism with 'what it is like to grow up not working in England'. He goes on:

> The under-class is that group which combines desolate living conditions and the lack of traditional bonds even of class with low skills and hopeless employment prospects. The result is cynicism towards the official values of a society bent on work and order. The under-class is not a revolutionary force, but one which will make its presence felt by crime, riots, and also by forming a volatile reserve army of militancy on either extreme of the political spectrum. It is an indictment of our prosperous societies, especially since a large number of those in the under-class are young.

Dahrendorf explains the prevalence of an under-class in Britain and the United States as resulting from 'the unusual plight' of their inner cities. He suggests that no measure to remedy this situation will be lastingly successful 'unless, at the very least, ways are found soon to make sure that every young person in the country has had some meaningful experience of training and activity by the time they reach their twenties'. Dahrendorf concludes his letter:

> If we do not succeed in including young citizens fully in our societies one must fear that there will be a frightening vacillation between situational violence and mindless law-and-order policies; a double threat which is as likely all over the free world as it is unattractive to the fan of liberty.[9]

What must it feel like to be a teenager with nothing to do, day after day, except wander round the city's shopping centres looking through their windows at enticing goods you can hardly imagine having the money to buy? Or how depressing, how damaging to self-esteem to live on an outer housing estate as someone now arrived in middle-age and know oneself to be a member of the long-term apparently unemployable unemployed. *Thatcher's?*

Health

On the evidence of environment, housing and employment alone it can hardly come as a surprise that the health of those who belong to the lower end of the Registrar General's class categories and who form the larger part of those living in the inner cities is considerably worse than those in the higher professional classes.

As we might expect, then, there are a number of major examples of health variation according to class in Britain today. Whether you take accidents as a basis for comparison, or respiratory disease, heart disease, cancer, or health in the first year of life or in retirement you will find the same story. There are drastic health inequalities along class lines. Out of every hundred thousand men aged 15—64 the direct age-standardized deathrate score (the higher the number, the higher your risk of early death) for university teachers is 287. For primary and secondary school teachers it is 396. For bricklayers' labourers it is 1644.[10]

The Black Report quoted above analysed these differentials in detail. It does not blame the National Health Service for them since their cause lies beyond its control. The report suggests that such factors as income, work, environment, education, housing, transport and general life-style are what make the difference. Good health depends on adequate conditions in these spheres, on home amenities and living standards for example, as much as on medical and nursing standards. Ironically, although the socially disadvantaged are in most need of the NHS the report makes it clear that the lower economic classes actually use it less and often receive less adequate treatment. As a result the report recommends a shift away from the modern primary medical definition of health (inherited from the thinking of Asclepius and his followers) as freedom from clinically ascertainable disease. This view of health was reinforced in the modern world by the Cartesian philosophy of the body as a machine and medical science as a kind of engineering process on it. The report stresses the existence of other concepts of health. For disciples of the goddess Hygeia it was rational social organization and individual behaviour which were all-important to human health. Implicit in this approach are the notions of vigour, well-being, and engagement with one's environment or community. It is an approach echoed by the World Health Organization's definition of health as 'a state of complete physical, mental and social wellbeing, and not merely the absence of disease or infirmity'. Such a social approach is bound to include concern for diet, fitness, immunization, health education and whatever is of importance to physical, cognitive or emotional growth.

Although the Black Report's recommendations for action were dismissed it is nevertheless difficult to argue with its description of the problem. Inner cities *are* places where mortality and morbidity rates are high, and they are likely to remain so while poor social conditions prevail.

The consequences of low income, overcrowding, pollution, cold and damp, lack of hygiene, inadequate means of communication (such as no telephone), and a lack of continuous care for children (for example in a one-parent family) are inevitably serious for health. They include much greater risk of respiratory disease and accidents, worse sight, less efficient hearing, skin disorders, the clustering of ill health in families and poor physical development. This in

itself makes inner city children more susceptible to illness.
And inadequately treated bouts of childhood sickness, as the
Court Report[11] put it, 'cast long shadows forward'.

A diet of crisps, sweets and biscuits compounds the
problem, and illustrates it. Parents may not understand the
relation between diet and health. Their general level of insight
about parenting may be severely limited and their emotional
freedom narrow. Many parents simply do not understand
what the basic conditions of human growth are. Autocratic or
over-permissive modes of parenting may predominate rather
than the more developmentally appropriate democratic ones.
The result is, in UPAs, a dimension of psychological
deprivation to be added to the others listed so far.

Education, racism and class

As a new curate at the Elephant and Castle, I went to visit a
local girls' secondary school. It came as a shock to be told by
the Head Teacher that she estimated the illiteracy rate
amongst leavers to be about 30%. I asked how she would
define illiteracy to which she replied: 'Someone who can't
read the Daily Mirror.' She told me that she estimated the
daily truancy rate at about 30% as well, caused mainly by
girls being forced to remain at home to look after younger
siblings or feeling they did not need to come to school since it
was unlikely to help them to get the job they wanted behind
the perfume counter or in hairdressing. That was in 1973.
Given the dramatic worsening of the employment prospects
facing young people since then it was only to be expected that
morale in schools and enthusiasm for schooling would
deteriorate. As *Faith in the City* puts it:

> Many pupils in UPA schools today are tragically aware of
> the world of *un*employment which confronts their families.
> We cannot over-stress the seriousness of this situation.
> The loss of hope and morale in many UPA schools borders
> on the catastrophic.(. . .) There is a sense in the UPAs of a
> progressively deteriorating environment for teachers and
> their pupils.[12]

Educational prospects well illustrate inner city disadvantage.
The inner city is a different world. Many middle-class people

In 1939 at a Council Sch... in ... with whose catchment area inclded a ...tish... ... area we had almost no 100% illiteracy. why?

don't think twice about their children's chances at GCSE. It is assumed they will be taken and passed. Independent schools pride themselves on the high percentage of their pupils (perhaps 75%) who go on to university.

Children in ordinary UPA schools have a 0.003% prospect of going to university. The gulf fixed between social classes is a canyon. British people tend not to notice this. We are used to it. The deep-rootedness of our class system makes it invisible to us. But if the task is to observe its pastoral consequences in the inner city, the statistics appear in stark relief. What had been taken for granted suddenly appears appalling. *The old Grammar schools did little to further this flaw*

For children from ethnic minorities the situation is far worse, as the House of Commons Select Committee's Report on Racial Disadvantage[13] showed. The report admitted, 'It has long been clear that we have not got ethnic minority education right.' Lord Scarman's Report commented:

> The under-achievement of West Indian children at school has been well chronicled recently in the Rampton Report. . . . I have received evidence from many organizations and individuals pointing to the failure of black youth to acquire sufficiently early the skills of language and literacy, and to the sense of disappointment and frustration which at least some black parents and children feel in the education system.[14]

Although black people make up only about 4% of our society the great majority of them live in UPAs. Ethnicity is used as an indicator of deprivation by *Faith in the City* since so many black people are concentrated in UPAs 'in poorly paid jobs, bad housing and unemployment. They are the people who carry a disproportionate share of the burden of adapting to the recent economic recession and industrial re-organization in Britain.'[15] The experience of racism is a daily event for black people, although it may be covertly signalled. An elderly West Indian woman without any trace of a chip on her shoulder once reluctantly admitted to me, 'It's the way the sparkle goes out of their eyes when they talk to you.' Often it is far from covert. In Tottenham we woke up one morning in 1983 to find more than a hundred yards of graffiti daubed along buildings and walls. Some of the worst were opposite

the front gates of a primary school and for three or four
weeks before the Council cleared them, young mothers
collecting their children from school had to read in letters a
foot high, 'Slums for Filthy Wogs', 'Burn Black Babies' and
'Set Fire to Blacks'.

These are the ways in which black people encounter racism.
They meet it in looking for housing or employment. They met
it when they first came to church in the 1950s and have met
it ever since. It stands as a rebuke to the witness of the
Church of England that when thousands of immigrants
proudly presented their confirmation cards from Jamaica or
Barbados they received only a cold shoulder from the
Christian family that they naively believed themselves to be
members of. Nor, thirty years later, can the Church of
England or the other historic churches feel satisfied that the
situation has improved. While in the West Indies the majority
of Christians belonged to the historic churches, in England in
the Eighties it is the Black-led churches who attract the
greater number of black Christians. In 1986 the Southwark
Diocese Race Relations Commission published findings from
a parish survey which showed the magnitude of the failure by
many clergy to take racism seriously. And *Faith in the City*
received evidence from the Commission for Racial Equality
that members of minority groups still feel 'ignored and
relegated to the peripheries of church life'.[16]

In our society now black people are available to be cast in
the role of an identifiable, recognizable and persecutable
minority. From the perspective of a sociologist, British society
'has shown a singular inability to cope with its new citizens'.[17]
Yet this is seen by many as the 'single most difficult and
important task' facing us today, and one whose neglect has
already proved to be a source of serious social unrest.

For Ralf Dahrendorf the issues of race and class are
superimposed. He says: 'Race riots and class riots are almost
indistinguishable.' This seems to me to be true. Between
1979 and 1985 I was the Vicar of the Parish of Holy Trinity,
Tottenham where I had plenty of opportunity to see the
groundswell of social deprivation and racial disadvantage
which erupted into the shocking Tottenham riot in which PC
Blakelock was hacked to death. In the immediate aftermath I
wrote to *The Times* whose leading article on the subject had

seemed to me to express perfectly a middle-class inability to grasp the significance of what was happening:

> Your perspective is that of a hardening heart. . . . Are you not aware that each injured policeman symbolizes the feelings of the underclass towards a self-satisfied, complacent middle class who appear to have everything when they have nothing? For six years I have walked the streets of Tottenham amazed that men, women and youths were prepared to live in such a brutalized environment without boiling over. Their hopelessness and frustration are inevitable and natural for those with eyes to see or who bother to look.
>
> Most middle-class people haven't the faintest idea what it must feel like to live on the Broadwater Farm Estate with no money, no job and, apparently, no prospect of one. Inner city life is hell. And the question must be pressed: What is middle-class Britain going to do about it?
>
> At the moment, whether you look at health, housing, environment, education, child care, care of the elderly or social and community work generally the answer rings back, 'very little'.
>
> I don't want the part of me which sympathizes with the rioters to get bigger, but how can it not when society generally seems not to care about the unacceptable quality of life which being born in a British inner city imposes on its captives?[18]

The social context

The last decade has been characterized by a great deal of political ferment and controversy. Social commentators, be they bishops or academics, have found themselves increasingly drawn into political wrangling. *Faith in the City* itself was accused by many of having made recommendations coloured by a political bias inappropriate for a church document. But social analysis can of course be seen as inextricably linked with political analysis. For example, it is impossible to gain an understanding of the drastic social changes which have affected the inner city in recent years without taking account of their social and political context.

Indeed, for the churches to make responsible pastoral
strategies to meet human needs they must look at the likely
consequences of social changes and political policies. The
environment of the inner city has been deteriorating since the
1970s, and the seeds of this decline were sown decades
before.[19] In the early nineteenth century capital was invested
in local family firms. Often only exploitative management
could survive because generosity towards the worker simply
led to bankruptcy. This rather than maliciousness led to the
brutal conditions of Dickensian Britain some of whose
victims' progeny now inhabit the inner cities. Nineteenth-
century capitalism simply could not bring affluence. Labour-
intensive production could not allow workers to share the
spoils. There was just not enough to go round – though there
was always the hope that there might be.

The response of the minimalist nineteenth-century state to
this economy was laissez-faire politics. For example, despite
the continued flourishing of corn, wheat and livestock the
British Government would not intervene, when the Irish
potato crop failed, to enable the Irish poor to buy these cash
crops. The export prices were too good. So fifty per cent of
the country either fled the country or died.

The early twentieth century saw an amelioration in the lot
of the workforce. Organizations could cope with some of the
demands of the new unions without going out of business,
especially where their capital was nationally consolidated.
Meanwhile technology brought a better balance of capital and
labour, which laid the foundations of a consumer society.
Henry Ford even produced a car his own workers could buy.
This new economic structure needed a political response for
it to work, a national banking system and the stock market,
for example. A social welfare state became possible. Politics
could increasingly be directed to the common good. Across
the Atlantic the 'American Dream' flourished. In Britain Mr
Macmillan could say at a garden fête in Bedford in 1957:
'Most of our people have never had it so good.'

The social and political turmoil of the 1980s, so strongly
felt in the UPAs, cannot be understood apart from the
realization that this more benevolent phase of industrial
capitalism is rapidly being taken over by a new and bleaker
one. For people over twenty this comes as something of a

shock since there was a pleasant stability about the old order which we had imagined continuing indefinitely.

What are some of the features of the new phase? Two facts stand out. As the world industrializes, capital is increasingly becoming transnational. And technology is becoming capital-intensive, that is, using less labour in relation to capital. Beyond these shifts lie new and perhaps menacing forms of social organization.

Transnational capital outflanks labour in two ways. First, it can be moved rapidly to the country in which the return is greatest. A strong national labour union, for example, can lead to the capital in that industry being removed to another country where labour is cheaper. Secondly, transnational capital facilitates industrial diversification. One company can own a newspaper, properties in different places, an aviation company, farming interests and a chain of supermarkets. If one of its concerns is jeopardized by organized labour it can be subsidized from the profits in other areas or simply abandoned.

Capital-intensive technology presents an even grimmer prospect. It means, quite simply, that fewer workers are needed for the job. And so, in recent years, we begin to face structural unemployment with the marginalization of perhaps one third of society into a new under-class quite unable to participate in the main economy. In 1981, in Britain, more than one and half million children were living at or below supplementary benefit level. And should the Government publish more recent statistics, the figure would rise dramatically.

The political ramifications of these social and economic developments have serious consequences for the poor in society. Low wages, high unemployment and social service cutbacks will be the price paid for successful performance on the international economic stage, and it is likely that such objectives will only be achieved by increasingly coercive and authoritarian styles of government.

Looked at in this light, the Government's peremptory rejection of the Black Report's recommendations to revitalize the NHS at a possible cost of £4,848m,[20] and its instant hostility to the proposals of *Faith in the City* are readily understood.

When there are lots of industrial workers we are told its bad for their health!

Those who have no choice but to continue living in our inner cities can clearly expect little relief from social and political institutions in the foreseeable future for their feelings of anxiety, hopelessness and anger and that is a measure of the immensity of the pastoral task which faces the Churches in urban priority areas.

Notes

1. *Faith in the City*, p. 229.
2. ibid, p. 261.
3. Lord Scarman, *The Brixton Disorders 10—12 April 1981*, HMSO.
4. See P. Golding, ed., *Excluding the Poor*, CPAG 1986.
5. See *Homelessness An Act of Man*, National Federation of Housing Associations 1987.
6. P. Harrison, *Inside the Inner City*, Penguin 1983, p. 183.
7. Figures derived from DHSS and DE statistics.
8. Scarman, 6.28.
9. R. Dahrendorf, letter to *The Times*, 3 June 1985.
10. P. Townsend and N. Davidson (eds.), *Inequalities in Health: The Black Report*, Penguin 1982, table 42.
11. Circular HC(78)5, *Health Services Development: Court Report on Child Health Services*, January 1978.
12. *Faith in the City*, pp. 295—6.
13. House of Commons Home Affairs Committee, 'Racial Disadvantage vol.1: Report with Minutes of Proceedings', Session 1980—81, 5th Report (HMSO), para. 130.
14. Scarman 2.18.
15. *Faith in the City*, p. 10.
16. ibid, p. 96.
17. This and the two following quotations from R. Dahrendorf, *On Britain*, BBC 1982, p. 67f.
18. J. N. A. Bradbury, letter to *The Times*, 10 October 1985.
19. In the analysis of this decline I am indebted to J. Holland and P. Henriot SJ, *Social Analysis*, New York, Orbis 1985, pp. 64—86. See also J. Atherton, *Faith in the Nation*, SPCK 1988.
20. This was the figure estimated by Sir George Young's Department (DHSS) and which he quoted in the House of Commons, 31 July 1981.

TWO

The Inner World of Feelings and Beliefs

And when he drew near and saw the city he wept over it, saying, 'Would that even today you knew the things that make for peace.'

Luke 19.41

The emotional cost

All personal emotional and psychological problems have a social and environmental context. Psychiatrists can predict a person's mental health better on the basis of his or her social setting than from a clinical diagnosis. The fact that a woman has hallucinations now tells a psychiatrist little about how she will be in ten years time. But if she is a single parent of thirty living in relative poverty with a family history involving crime and emotional disturbance a prediction about her mental health in ten years, assuming no change of environment, is easier to make.[1]

Stress, a major cause of both physical and mental illness, can be maintained by chronic environmental factors. And where those environmental factors are likely to remain constant the probability is that the individual will continue to be adversely affected by stress. In the terminology of modern psychology *stress* is used to refer to body/mind changes brought about by *stressors,* i.e. life events and circumstances which pressurize an individual. Up to a point the human organism copes with stressors through the compensatory systems such as regulation of the heart or our ability to sweat. But if the external pressure of stressor-events and circumstances reaches a level which the body's adaptive system cannot deal with stress occurs and produces physical and/or emotional damage.

19

Early research into stress was able to predict the likelihood of a heart attack within eighteen months by adding up the score of stressors allocated to different life events. The death of a spouse scored 100, divorce 73, personal illness 53, a holiday 13, Christmas 12 and so on. Beyond a certain total the risk increased. More recent research differentiates between three categories of stressor. Unique *life events,* such as bereavement or giving birth to a child are one kind. *Daily hassles* are another; these would include getting the children to school, collecting them, preparing a meal, all under pressure of time. *Chronic stressors,* such as poverty, long-term unemployment or under-nourishment are the third.

In calculating a person's vulnerability to stress it is necessary to take all three categories into account. It is also important to assess how the various stressors are being *perceived* by that person. People respond to stressors differently according to circumstance. And early research into life events ignored their perceived consequences. It would not have given a high stressor rating to a trip to the shops. But if someone under financial strain must face the hassle of frightening underpasses and dangerous traffic and manage three young children round the supermarket the stressor score may be very high.

The cumulative effect of the multiple chronic stressors in an inner city environment can be highly significant. It is this which helps to explain the pervasive sense of wretchedness which can sometimes be felt in even the most modern and attractive inner city housing estate. It is a wretchedness which baffles the outsider. Why *should* so much unhappiness seem to lie behind these front doors when the gardens are attractively landscaped and the flats well designed and new? People might easily feel they could enjoy living there.

What such a superficial view does not notice is the reciprocal influence continuously transacted between the unhappy individuals on the estate and their environment from the very start of life. In fact this amounts to more than the impact of the environment on a person and *vice versa,* because everyone plays a significant part in their own self-development. For example, if an infant smiles on being picked up the smile affects the parent's next reaction. The parent reacts differently if the infant cries rather than smiles.

These patterns of interaction plus mutual influence and self development are described by psychologists as *transactions*. They can be represented diagrammatically:

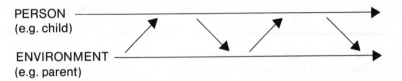

The *parallel lines* are life lines. The *transverse lines* show the transactions between person and environment. A person influences his or her own development in so far as the way he or she reacts modifies the *next* reaction from the environment. If the pattern of transactions in a person's life goes wrong or is never creative they will be continually susceptible to stress as long as there is no change in the environment of their transactions. Statistics show that many people get better fast during a short stay in a psychiatric hospital. But they suffer speedy relapse when they get home because the transactions of that environment caused their illness and continue to maintain it. Sameroff's comprehensive review of the research, published in the mid-seventies, showed that the *whole* transaction must be taken into account rather than just one of its aspects (the behaviour and attitudes of the parents, for example).[2] This has led to something of a revolution in social work, and to a good deal of retraining. It was discovered that professional intervention could make matters worse. It was sometimes found, for example, that much more serious child abuse than had occurred hitherto happened soon after the first visit of a social worker. Even the modest suggestion of a health visitor to attend antenatal classes can easily be heard by a pregnant mother to imply 'because otherwise you'll be no good'.

The cumulative force of inner city environmental factors frequently produces disastrous transactions between child and parent or person and person. One-parent families are greatly at risk because lack of resources often leads to *some* kind of starvation, if only neglect. Television, for example, can be a forceful and destructive child minder since the inner city primary school child who watches thirty or more hours of television a week actually needs that time for *development,* for conversation with a parent, for example.

Research points to an alarming differential between the incidence of depression among working class mothers, compared with the rest of the population. Something like 30% of working class mothers have been found to require help from the professional agencies for this condition and the consequences of disabling bouts of depression in mothers may be catastrophic for their children's development.

Sheila, for example, is the casualty of such an upbringing. Sheila is twenty. She has a son of six months. Yet twice since his birth she has had to be hospitalized for attempted suicide. Why? Because the child's father left her for another woman when the baby came. Because she has been moved four times into different bed and breakfast accommodation. Because she seems unable to manage on £31.45 a week. Because her baby screams incessantly. Because her neighbours hassle her. Because the Social Services Department threatens to take her baby away. But above all because she herself has never experienced the security of a mother who was sufficiently free from depression and self-disdain to pass on any confidence to her daughter.

The evidence from psychology shows just how far a person's maturation is dependent on the quality of their early relationships. As adults we inherit a psychological disposition as well as a bodily one. The picture of the world we possess, the structure of our personality, depends on intimate contact with others. The relationships of our infancy may have enabled us to trust or else, if our needs were constantly not met, have left us with a picture of the world as untrustworthy and others as unreliable. The 'good enough' mother (in D. W. Winnicott's phrase[3]) is one who holds the infant safely both physically and emotionally so that the child is not overwhelmed by painful feelings such as helplessness, rage, fear or guilt but learns to manage anxieties. 'Contained' by the mother, the child learns to internalize sufficient safety to allow his or her further psychic development.

As well as being a container, a parent needs also to be a thinker for the child: someone, that is, who not only tolerates the child's experience but who gives it meaning by thinking about it. W. R. Bion, who first described this process, showed how a child who could internalize the mind of his mother was himself able to learn to think.[4] But a child who has never experienced the care of a 'good enough' mother, will be less able to be a 'good enough' parent. Parents need to be sufficiently confident and free from anxiety, sufficiently in touch with and in charge of their own feelings to sustain their role. Clearly where a parent or parents are carrying the stress of chronic poverty, their relationships will be at risk.

All the wretchedness, anguish, depression and misery so pervasive in the inner city can be characterized as an overwhelming sense of powerlessness. It is the denial of that most profound of human needs, a feeling of having some control over one's life, that the inner city environment denies and frustrates with such destructive and costly results. Overcrowded housing, Local Authority bureaucracy, being unable to get something mended, having insufficient money to buy what advertisements offer, poor prospects of employment, a health service which operates more like passport control, inappropriate schools preparing children for a bleak future, against the back-drop of emotional deprivation, fear, high crime and physical squalor—all this combines to vitiate that sense of control so vital to self-esteem, so essential to health and development. It produces instead an unbearable sense of *being controlled,* of being a victim.

A bewildering array of belief

Conventional Religion

Conventional Christianity is credal. It offers orthodox beliefs, calling them doctrine. It is also both biblical and liturgical. The source book of the faith is the Bible and its worship makes use of time-honoured symbols expressed in liturgy. All this is problematic for the inner city. Most people who live there have never had any regular contact with the institutional church, and neither did their parents or grandparents. Researchers who have attempted to study the nature of belief in the inner city have found it to be a complex and elusive phenomenon.

I discovered this for myself (as a curate at the Elephant and Castle) during my first baptism preparation. Until ordination my experience of discussing baptism had been confined to college seminars and I was ill-prepared for my first baptism visit. 'How', I asked, 'do you feel about answering the question, "Do you believe and trust in God the Father who made the world?"'—and there was an embarrassed silence. At last the father of the family answered on behalf of all: 'Well', he said, 'it's a bit strong innit?'

The inner city, however specific its culture, inevitably shares the *materialistic outlook* of the wider culture in which it is set: 'That basic reality is material and all mental and spiritual facts are parasitic on this has become the unexamined assumption underlying the world view of most educated western people, and has been through them diffused into popular culture.'[5] An expression of such metaphysics in the inner city might be, 'When you're gone, you're gone'. To be a Christian in this climate is to claim the *opposite* of what people generally believe. It is to presuppose a fundamental *spiritual* reality and to see the physical universe as an expression of this underlying spiritual reality.

So for many modern people Christian faith is not built on plausible foundations. The general and deeply ingrained assumption today is that when you have taken away matter you have taken away existence. This is what death shows so harrowingly.

The present attitude towards belief tends to be one of *pluralism.* People feel that one particular religion is hardly likely to contain the whole truth. You should be free to 'shop around', and discover a religion which is 'right for you'. In the inner city's multicultural environment mosques and gurdwaras are as much to be expected as churches and police stations. The faith they represent meets with respect as well as suspicion. Their very presence suggests that God, if there is a God, may be found through a variety of religions. Pluralism undermines the 'taken-for-grantedness' of the traditional Christian outlook. It too, like materialism, works against the plausibility of belief. It erodes residual patterns of Christian faith.

But what has 'erosion'
was it ever there?

This erosion of traditional outlook is reinforced by our cultural emphasis on *individualism*. Popular individualism is unreceptive to the church's traditional teaching that individual beliefs go hand in hand with the powerful influences of culture, language and upbringing. Moreover, the essentially historical and biblical foundations of Christianity are increasingly at odds with the modern world-view. Today's shared assumptions tend to find the very grounds of Christian religion incredible.

Within the church institution there is such a widely *divergent interpretation of belief* and such pervasive controversy about its content and meaning that it is very hard to know what the church is *asking* for by way of belief. For the traditional Christian creeds do not address themselves to our modern pre-occupations. We are not straining to match our belief to fourth-century Neo-Platonism. We might like some guidance on how a Christian might be involved in politics; but the creeds are not interested in this and do not discuss it.

Can Scripture help? Certainly it can inspire us by its poetry and exhortation. We can be intrigued by its controversies and legal codes. Above all we can be stirred by its powerful stories and narratives. But as for helping us work out what we believe, it seems rather to make matters worse. It does not contain the kind of documents we need as a basis for the logical deduction of doctrine. The Bible is of course the unique primary source for the religion, but as soon as you ask 'Which religion?', 'A religion which believes precisely what?' you are faced with a huge problem. There is, in particular, the difficulty of interpreting a culture far removed from our own. For example it is not easy to tackle the question of whether or not 'Jesus is Lord', or whether or not 'God was in Christ reconciling the world to himself', if there is serious doubt as to what these statements mean. Unfortunately, most of the traditional concepts of Christian doctrine fall into this category; salvation; redemption; resurrection; incarnation; the Trinity; ascension; the Holy Spirit; together with heaven and hell, eternal life and so on.

Neither are the difficulties confined to the task of interpreting the past. Our present culture contributes its own stumbling blocks to making sense of faith. The problem of a

materialist outlook, already noted, works against the
cultivation of a sense of being a 'child of God', when that God
is Spirit. So do other forces. Christianity depends on its
corporate memory not just as its gateway to the past but as a
means of bringing that past into the present. People in the
past who experienced God as 'Lord' or 'king' need to be
replaced by living people in the next generation who
experience God in the same way. Religion doesn't just depend
on dusty documents which could be kept in a library. It needs
people to embody these ideas by the way they live their lives.

The corporate memory depends upon people doing this in
the same way across the generations. Our culture does not
encourage this, and the identity of Christian 'role performance'
(as the sociologists call it) is threatened as a result. It is then
difficult for those not reared within a strongly Christian
environment to grasp what Christian people *mean* by Saviour,
Christ or Holy Spirit. They may never have been exposed to a
person who could demonstrate in their lives the influence of
prayer to God, or seeking God's will. Equally, a particular
image, say, of God as 'our father', can lose its meaning if
someone has never known an equivalent human relationship
to match it. A child who has never known a father and has
been brought up in a situation where men were few and far
between may have a resistance to, or negative understanding
of, God if he is described as Father.

Common Religion

While conventional religion finds itself rendered increasingly
superfluous by the modern world-view, folk religion, with its
ingredients of fate, ghosts, superstition, luck, the occult,
clairvoyance and astrology is gaining credence. 'Folk' or
'common' religion can be defined as 'those beliefs and
practices of an overtly religious nature which are not under
the domination of a prevailing religious institution.'[6] Its scope
can even include the existence of God and prayer. This is a
significant feature of life in the inner city. Clearly, pastoral
care in a UPA must take account of it since it powerfully
affects the hopes, expectations and attitudes (positive or
negative) that people have towards the churches.

In the book *Inner City God*, G. Davie comments: 'Common religion is by nature thematic and not systematic; it is made up of a large number of separate elements which do not necessarily form a coherent whole. An individual may well contradict himself in the course of an interview about his beliefs.' It is a messy, contradictory blend. Davie quotes one individual who, when asked in a survey, 'Do you believe in a God who can change the course of events on earth?' replied, 'No, just the ordinary one.'[7] Common religion separates belief from religious practice. As Davie goes on to say, 'It is clear that among working-class people in particular, church-going is plainly not seen as a necessary part of Christianity.' Belief in God and leading a good life are equally stressed but for working class people 'regular church attendance is often bluntly categorised as hypocrisy'.[8]

On the contrary, according to another researcher, belief in common religion relates to *social* practice.[9] Geoffrey Ahern sees the notion 'belief' and its mirror 'disbelief' (as in the sense: 'He believes in the life-force') as belonging to the mental structuring of 'Western-influenced education'. It is bound up with a quest for middle-class personal identity. He concludes that it is a mistake to project this mentality into the inner city. For example, one of his respondents said, 'I do believe in Christmas' using the word 'believe' in a very different sense from believing in the life-force, in Jesus as the Son of God. Researchers stress, in general, the profoundly inarticulate nature of common religion and the very ambivalent nature of its relationship with conventional religion. For example, rites of passage such as weddings, christenings and burials are included in working class common religion but Church of England services are seen as 'them' rather than 'us'. Vicars, at least those who are visible in the community, are regarded as having a place, even an important one, whereas the Church of England and certainly Anglicanism often have a negative image. They tend to be identified with the authority of an alien world which, like political authority, is not entirely to be trusted and may be seen as hostile.[10]

Positive features

Despite the hope expressed in its title, *Faith in the City* states:

> It is our considered view that the nation is confronted by a *grave and fundamental injustice* in the UPAs. The facts are officially recognised, but the situation continues to deteriorate and requires urgent action. No adequate response is being made by government, nation or church. There is barely even widespread discussion.[11]

Lord Scarman's report, too, is unrelenting in its attack on the social conditions of Britain's inner cities in general and Brixton in particular. He concludes by saying that 'to ignore the existence of these factors is to put the nation in peril'. These are strong words from a British judge. Nevertheless Lord Scarman allows himself a glimmer of optimism. It is this:

> There is much in Brixton, and it is a tribute to its people that this is so, which is positive and creative: one only has to walk the streets to appreciate the vigour and the liveliness of its multi-racial society. Many people who live in Brixton have emphasized to me its positive features — not least the generally amicable relations between its black and white inhabitants — and their pleasure in living there.[12]

We need to make a simple, clear distinction between appalling social conditions and the human beings who endure them. The environment may do its worst and yet leave innumerable instances in which resilient people rise above their circumstances and display every known human virtue including oversized portions of generosity, humour, warmth, friendliness, self-sacrifice for others' benefit — in a word, love.

I shall never forget the harassed woman who poured out to me her venomous feelings towards everyone and everything for about ten minutes. I sympathized since she was truly in a wretched situation with little to alleviate it. When she had finished her tirade she paused, gave me a long look and said, with the ghost of a twinkle: 'Mind you, I'd never say nothing against nobody. I'd give my worsest enemy a cup of tea.' Whatever redemption means, that remark conveyed something of it. So did the generosity and humour of an elderly parishioner, a woman of very slender means, who shuffled into church during a collection for Christian Aid. 'Silver and gold have I none,' she scowled, 'still,' as she fumbled in her bag, 'I didn't say I never 'ad no pound notes' and she put one in.

Anyone who has lived or worked in the inner city has a string of similar anecdotes. It is important to emphasize the seemingly indomitable character of many people. It is as if the brutalized environment does not exist for them. To take one extreme example, people can be sitting in a room which by any description would have to be called a squalid slum and apparently not notice the smell of decaying animal faeces and rooms uncleaned for months. And in this unsavoury scene the human atmosphere can be bright and merry.

Many people *are* happy, and neither ask for nor seek any change in their lives. In his important book *The People of Providence*[13] Tony Parker lets a cross section of people who live on an inner city housing estate speak for themselves. The result is vivid — a rounded human portrait of how people face up to poverty. The book adds an authentic, often poignant biographical dimension to the sociological surveys on contemporary urban life. One interviewed lady, a pensioner widow of seventy-seven with a self-confessed weakness for peppermint creams, summed up her life like this:

> I'm a lucky woman I would say, I've got everything I need: if I'm ill or anything there's always one of the children or grandchildren will come over and see that I'm alright. There's nothing I need and nothing I want for; I have a nice regular life and I'm perfectly happy with it. So long as things go as they should, it seems to me you shouldn't ask for more. My life's ordered and content.[14]

In this and the other transcripts the blend of inner strength and fragility which determines a person's response to their situation quickly becomes evident. It is beyond analysis — the gateway to philosophical questions about the human spirit which this book cannot begin to approach.

In my experience there tends to be a greater sense of human solidarity than exists elsewhere. Perhaps it stems from the need to club together against the common enemy of a harsh life. In London it is a solidarity with the memory of summer hop-picking in Kent, street parties for the coronation, and the corporate suffering of the blitz. Whatever its history there is now a famous neighbourliness in the inner city which has by no means been broken down by extensive redevelopment and the building of many new estates. The obverse side of the pressure which keeps people indoors and uninvolved is a readiness to talk easily with anyone, known or unknown. Emotions can be shared with an immediacy that would throw a respectable member of the middle class into shock. Newcomers to the city soon learn. One lady in the congregation at the Elephant and Castle had no hesitation whatever in forcibly pointing out to me, after one of my first sermons as a curate: 'I thought it was bloody awful and I wish I'd stayed at home and done my knitting.' There is a tremendous freedom from the constricting social conventions of the middle class.

Comfortably-off people from the shires, when visiting their linked parishes in the inner city will frequently express their admiration at how well the city congregation's members know each other and, in particular, the ease with which they can share their feelings. There is the feel of an extended family which is gloriously unrestricted by tight boundaries. Warmth between people is generously and uninhibitedly expressed. Nor is this openness confined to talking and the sharing of feelings. On his rounds a parish priest is constantly regaled with the stories of those grateful for the caring, neighbourly acts they have received. Sadness at the loneliness of the elderly or the isolation and frustration of the single mother must go hand in hand with rejoicing at the innumerable acts of kindness which neighbours offer each other, especially those in need. There is a quality of care and a pervasive and stubborn retention of good humour, and a sense of humour, which is precious indeed and from which the rest of society can learn. It goes without saying that the virtues described here can be found wherever there are human beings and not just in designated urban priority areas.

Inner cities offer a broad and generally tolerated diversity of life-style. This applies equally to private life and life on the streets. Gay clergy, for example, tend to find much greater acceptance within the culture of the inner city than elsewhere in the country. More visibly, there is the sheer delight of a cosmopolitan community in which religious, social and cultural differences add positively and interestingly to the life of all. A multi-ethnic community enjoys a variety of features and customs which can be mutually enriching and life-enhancing.

There has been a broadening in styles of eating, worshipping, dressing, socializing and music-making. High Streets are transformed by the appearance of an Indian corner shop selling fresh samosas, a West Indian butcher selling the ingredients for goat curry, and an Afro-Caribbean grocer displaying fresh coriander, sweet potatoes and enormous water melons. Children in school learn something about Diwali and Ramadan. They become able to respect and participate in the celebrations of their Moslem, Hindu and Sikh friends.[15] Silk saris and African cotton prints are as commonplace as blue jeans. Reggae has influenced the history of music as much as the blues. Mosques, gurdwaras and Hindu temples bear witness to ancient traditions of human wisdom which hint at the spiritual moribundity of individualistic western secularism.

These cultural strengths nourish what was in danger of becoming a tired complacency—a passive, unenquiring, limpness of spirit, due to the fact that working-class people, having become accustomed to their place in the British scheme of things, had also become stuck in their ways. There were, and still are, alarming signs of apathy, a lack of imagination and a collective weariness of attitude. But this tendency is challenged by the ethnic minorities. They introduce a diversity and a vitality which, when not thwarted by racism, contributes hugely to the quality of life in the inner city.

Lastly, and elusively, there is a *drama* about the inner city which many people find potent and attractive. From the banter of the street market, the honky-tonk of the piano in a pub on a Saturday night, children playing in the streets, the fast pace of the shoppers, the soap opera enacted on the buses, the battle to achieve some community goal or defend some community right, to the excitement of a big football match, there is a bracing rawness, a resilience of spirit and a compelling dynamism in this theatre of life.

Nothing here makes right the environmental conditions of

Britain's inner cities. The Archbishop's Commission on Urban Priority Areas and the other reports have made their recommendations to the nation and it remains to be seen whether or not they will be responded to adequately. At the moment this looks unlikely. The Archbishop's Commission concludes: 'We have found faith in the city.' The task of the Churches is to act on this faith for the advance of God's Kingdom and the pastoral care of his children who live there.

Notes

1. An example given by Professor Sims (University of Leeds) in a lecture at the University of Birmingham Pastoral Studies Conference, 1984.
2. A. J. Sameroff, 'Early Influences on Development: Fact or Fantasy?', in *Merrill–Palmer Quarterly* 21, 1975, pp. 267–94.
3. See M. Davis and D. Wallbridge, *Boundary and Space: An Introduction to the work of D. W. Winnicott,* Penguin 1983, p. 45f.
4. See I. Salzberger-Wittenberg, G. Henry and E. Osborne, *The Emotional Experience of Learning and Teaching,* Routledge and Kegan Paul 1983, p. 60f.
5. J. A. Baker, 'Carried about by Every Wind?: The Development of Doctrine', in the Report of Doctrine Commission of the Church of England, *Believing in the Church,* SPCK 1981, p. 263. The discussion of 'Conventional Religion' in this chapter owes much to this report as a whole.
6. Robert Towler's definition (see his *Homo Religiosus: Sociological problems in the study of religion,* Constable 1974, ch. 8), quoted in G. Davie, 'The nature of belief in the inner city' in G. Ahern and G. Davie, *Inner City God,* Hodder and Stoughton 1987, p. 34.
7. ibid., p. 39.
8. ibid., p. 55.
9. ibid., p. 91.
10. ibid., pp. 86–122.
11. *Faith in the City,* p. xv.
12. Lord Scarman, *The Brixton Disorders 10–12 April 1981*, HMSO, 2.33.
13. T. Parker, *The People of Providence: A housing estate and some of its inhabitants,* Hutchinson 1983.
14. ibid., p. 356.
15. See R. Hooker and C. Lamb, *Love the Stranger: Ministry in Multi-Faith Areas,* SPCK 1986, for a complete discussion of the pastoral questions in relation to this issue.

THREE

The Church of England and the Inner City

'Come, let us return and visit the brethren in every city where we proclaimed the word of the Lord, and see how they are doing.'

Acts 15.36

The essential structure of parish pastoral care in eighteenth-century England had changed little since the Middle Ages. Like its medieval forerunner it was both compact and inclusive. For some 500 years the parish priest had been charged with the cure of souls of all his parishioners, whatever their social rank. The Fourth Lateran Council of 1215 stated explicitly the requirement that each parishioner make his or her confession once a year or face church banishment and refusal of burial. And it required this confession to be made to the *local* priest.[1] Only with his permission could the confession be made to an outside priest. Such a regulation predicated a parish of modest and proportionate numbers.

400 years later the Ordinal of the *Book of Common Prayer* continued to assume that a single individual would be able to discharge the pastoral duties of the parish priest: 'Never cease your labour, your care and diligence, until you have done all that lieth in you. . . . to bring *all* such as . . . shall be committed to your charge, unto that agreement in the faith and knowledge of God . . .' (my italics). Little changed in the next 200 years. George Herbert advised his parson 'upon the afternoons in the weekdays . . . sometimes to visit in person, now one quarter of his parish now another.'[2] If pastoral practice in the eighteenth century sometimes fell short of this ideal, this was no doubt due to the fact that at a time when

romantic!   33

less than 10% of the population were city-dwellers, 'where the clergyman was resident, the communal nature of the small isolated rural community did not make it necessary to visit the homes of his people to be acquainted with them.'[3]

By the start of the present century all this had changed irrevocably. The industrial revolution of the preceding 150 years had led to unforeseen and cataclysmic social upheaval which moved large masses of the labour force from the country into the cities. By 1900, 40% of the population were living in cities of more than 100,000 inhabitants, and a further 20% in towns of more than 20,000 people.[4] The institutions which had adequately sustained pastoral care in parishes for so long were swiftly undermined by the pace of these events, although the Victorian Church did in fact respond with some vigour. It provided schools, Sunday schools, temperance campaigns and charitable relief. Churches were also built: 600 in urban areas between 1824 and 1884.[5]

The ancient parishes were swamped nevertheless. St Mary's Lambeth, for example, had 139,000 parishioners in 1853.[6] In 1851 the first census of church attendance had revealed that half the nation were non-churchgoers, the urban poor and working class being the largest social group amongst them. Within a few years of living in the city habits of churchgoing tended to be lost, never to return. The 1902/3 census of church attendance in London showed that, among adults, only about 4% of the urban poor went to church. In 1985, in average UPA parishes of 10,500 people, the figure is 0.85% (1.4% nationally).[7] This is the dilemma facing the Church of England in the last quarter of the twentieth century; to abandon the charge of the Ordinal or to minister somehow to 10,000, sometimes 30,000, parishioners.

This is the situation I faced on being ordained to a parish at the Elephant and Castle in South London in 1973. I was profoundly shocked. It was an experience for which five years of theological training at Oxford and Cuddesdon had scarcely prepared me. I was overwhelmed by the scale of human need I discovered and was made impotent by the size of the task. Confronted by a suicidal man during the first month of my curacy, whose case for death as the only escape available from a future of unrelieved wretchedness seemed perfectly convincing, I was made painfully aware of the inadequacy of my theological equipment. What could *I* say to a lonely old man who really did have nothing to live for, about the nature of God's love? I felt the same with disturbed children, drug addicts, the deeply depressed and many other kinds of parishioner. I began to feel that only a fool would preach the Church's God at the Elephant and Castle. My own search to come to terms with what pastoral care in the inner city could mean had begun.

After three years at the Elephant and Castle I spent a second three years in the inner city but with the Jesuits in New York City. Living in a Jesuit residence in the South Bronx taught me the grim realities of life in an American urban ghetto. The Bronx was as burnt out in places as the City of London after the Second World War. And the level of violence was terrifying, with stabbings and shootings as commonplace as English drizzle. The New York Jesuits were involved in an impressive breadth of ministry from running a University to a subway chaplaincy and parish work in the toughest areas. From them I learned to relate my spirituality more securely to my personality. But I also learned something which at the Elephant and Castle I had not seen. Each summer the Jesuits organized a 'Higher Achievement Program', an intensive training for Junior School children bussed into a Jesuit High School from areas like Harlem and the notoriously poor Lower East Side of Manhatten. Teaching on this programme taught me the importance for pastoral care of intervention in the structures which maintain poverty and introduced me to the political complexity of attempting to do this.

In 1979 I returned to a British UPA parish of 25,000 people and a large West Indian community in Tottenham, North London, this time as Vicar, and spent six years there. It was as far from George Herbert's vision of the country parish as it is possible to be. During this time the parish taught me to see the potential of a congregation for corporate care and action. In 1985 I moved to my present job as tutor in pastoral theology at a theological college. Here my role includes assisting future ministers to prepare realistically for their work in parishes as they are and in a society where more than seven million people live in urban priority areas.[8] It is a training which places importance on understanding, in the light of the gospel, the issues and implications raised by the inner city.

In my experience during the fifteen years since my ordination the response of the Church of England, its clergy and its congregations to the stark and forbidding state of affairs confronting them can be roughly characterized by four recurring types. Which type will depend primarily on the church's historical background, its tradition of churchmanship, its resources and the style of its current incumbent.

The following portraits are an attempt to illustrate each of these types and in doing so to provide an overview of the predicament facing the Church in its pastoral mission in a UPA parish.

St Aloysius and All Incense

The church of St Aloysius and All Incense lies in a quiet side street of the parish. The parish boundary, half a mile to the east, is the arterial main road to the city centre. Next to the church stands the six-bedroomed Victorian vicarage, the largest house in the parish. Most of the parish consists of flats built during the 1950s and 60s as part of a slum clearance programme. There are still some streets of terraced housing. For the last ten years these have been occupied almost exclusively by black families. There is no industry in the parish, just a few corner shops, seven off-licences and two Indian take-aways. The parish population is 17,000.

St Aloysius is a 'Father Knows Best' church. Lay people, where they contribute at all, see themselves as 'helping Father'. Father Halo is generally known and loved as a devout and saintly figure, though, like anyone, he has his foes who currently include a militant group of young mothers who are furious that he will not allow their Toddlers Group to take place in his church hall. Father Halo has been parish priest for sixteen years. He is now assisted by Father Blenkinsop a newly-ordained young man from a sound theological college who, like his five curate predecessors, lives in that part of the vicarage known as 'the curate's flat'. Both Fathers are ably and comfortably looked after by Mrs Holly, a rather powerful lady whose stinging phrase 'Father's busy, you'll have to come back later' has been felt by many an enquiring parishioner, especially on a Tuesday which is Father's day off.

There are 108 people on the electoral roll at St Aloysius, and with the children there are often eighty or so for Parish Mass on Sundays at 9 a.m. What is in no doubt at all is the devotion of the eight faithful few. They come to everything. Early Mass, Evensong, Holy Hour, Benediction and Rosary. In fact they are so committed that they take upon themselves nearly the whole burden of church work. They organize the Sunday flowers, the tea rota, the laundry and all the chores of the sacristy. Father Halo and Father Blenkinsop, meanwhile, are free to follow their daily regimen. After early mass, morning office and meditation they take breakfast at 9 a.m. Then follows a division of labour. Sixty-three disabled, sick and elderly parishioners are accustomed to receiving the Holy Sacrament in their homes every week. Father Blenkinsop sees to this, using Monday, Wednesday and Friday mornings. Father Halo uses his mornings for parish administration, sermon preparation and study. Sometimes he has to take a funeral or attend a clergy meeting. Generally though he is grateful for Mrs Holly's buffering him from callers during the morning, despite pangs of guilt.

On Thursday mornings Father Blenkinsop takes assembly at one of the local infant schools. Then he visits at a large old people's home, one of three in the parish. It may seem that quite a lot of his time is used up on the elderly but there are an estimated 3500 isolated old people living in the parish, indeed the local social services team leader regards their plight as one of the most serious problems she faces. The vast majority of these can of course never be visited but Father Blenkinsop does what he can.

Otherwise, funerals permitting, the afternoon is given over to visiting. Father Halo is mildly proud of the fact that his 'pastoral list' is so long, nearly 1300 people. These are the names and addresses of parishioners with whom he has had pastoral contact over the years. It may have been through a funeral, a baptism (these are the most common), a marriage, or simply as the result of a parishioner calling on him for help, or a member of the congregation telling him of a neighbour in need. So there is no shortage of people for the

Fathers to visit in the afternoons. On the contrary, both priests tend to feel overwhelmed by this side of their ministry. Father Halo secretly thinks he visits more than any vicar in his deanery. But the distressing truth is that day after day he senses a perplexing mixture of gratitude for his visits, yes, and hostility that he visits so rarely.

There is also a second reason for distress. When he's honest Father Halo often feels a wearied, almost resentful, boredom during his visits. Father Halo *is* deeply committed to his visiting and to the people he meets. He would love to bring relief to their pain. Above all he would like them to share his own faith in God, to understand the grace which could be theirs through the Church. But over the years it has been so hard to get beyond the family photographs, the wingeing about where life hurts, the nasty neighbours or the hypocrisy of the man on television. His visits have a predictability which Father Halo now finds enervating. Not that he leaves God out in his visits. He always says a prayer before leaving and has often noticed how poignant this seemed to be for them both. But all his years of faithful visiting have only drawn a handful of people, maybe seven or so, into the congregational fold where he would wish them to be. And this hurts. Night after night he trudges home bringing his mixed feelings to God, the God who is his strength and his stay. Each morning he opens his soul to God with the sincere prayer that this day he may be a means of God's grace to those he will visit. Whatever pain it may cause him, Father Halo never abandons his belief in the rightness of visiting. His belief in God's love for all people is unshakeable, and as a priest it is his duty and privilege to show this as best he can.

Evenings are taken up with meetings. There's a confirmation class drawn from the local school. Father Blenkinsop takes this since Father Halo has lately become disheartened by the fact that every year the candidates lapse within weeks of their confirmation.

Evenings are also used for baptism preparation. Father Halo takes this very seriously. He believes it is quite wrong to allow a baptism without some prior instruction in the faith. He has always taken the hard-line approach that families wanting baptism must attend church for three months and come to three instruction evenings. Naturally many families are not prepared to do this and go elsewhere, but Father Halo has nevertheless found that it is this which sometimes *does* lead to new members of the congregation.

Then, in addition to the usual PCC meetings and Finance and Fabric Committees there is the Club Committee and the Mission Committee. The Club is a social centre in an old church hall. It offers a variety of activities including a weekly pensioners' lunch, bingo, monthly disabled club, a women's meeting and a bar. The whole enterprise has to be co-ordinated and managed, especially since there are continuous problems about lettings, and Father Halo is chairman of the committee. He likes to think of the Club as the one place where the church meets the world on its own terms. He drops in occasionally and wishes it were more often. He always encourages baptism and wedding couples to visit it. Father Blenkinsop is a regular, and hundreds of parishioners call in over the year. No-one, Father Halo feels, could accuse St Aloysius of only offering pie in the sky. He sees the Club as his means of what he calls 'pre-evangelism'.

The other church meeting is the Mission Committee. This group has two tasks. It organizes a parish mission every three years, and it organizes the 'Holy Week Tableau' every year. The parish mission involves a lot of work. A leaflet is distributed to every house and flat in the parish detailing the times of the 'open lectures and discussion'. The talks are given by a visiting priest, or (better still), a bishop. During the week there is also an 'open' party to which anyone can come. Last time the mission was particularly aimed at the West Indian community living in the terraced housing and a black Pentecostalist preacher was invited to be one of the main speakers. The 'Holy Week Tableau' demands less work. Every year a lorry-mounted tableau of the crucifixion tours the streets on Good Friday witnessing to the parish and Father Halo is often told how touching his parishioners find the spectacle.

No portrait of St Aloysius could be complete without some comment on the preaching. For Father Halo this has high priority. It is a place to teach and to proclaim. Father Halo is a gifted preacher. Like his ministry through the Club, his sermons are rooted in the world. Father Halo therefore pays particular attention to social issues. He has recently

preached forcibly on the iniquity of unemployment,
irresponsible abortion legislation, the decline in educational
standards, the erosion of family life and the need for society
to maintain strong law and order. These issues are not
irrelevant in his parish. Unemployment is 30% and very high
indeed for school leavers. There are high rates of family
break-up and innumerable single-parent families. And there
is a seriously worrying increase in youth crime, vandalism
and drug addiction. Father Halo takes the view that the
church *must* speak out clearly on these matters so that for
Christians faith can be kept pure and the gospel not harmed.

The Church of St Paul and the Holy Table

Caricatures are unfair. The wit who described the
congregation of the Church of St Paul and the Holy Table as
all having 'thick black glasses, polyester suits and fat floppy
leather-covered bibles with gilt edges' was exaggerating.
Certainly the vicar, Mr Surefaith, conforms to this description
but his parishioners are a little less stereotyped. Although
Holy Table parish is adjacent to St Aloysius and despite a
great deal in common socio-economically you would hardly
believe the two church ministries were those of one
denomination.

The only funerals ever officiated at by Mr Surefaith are
those of the card-carrying members of his own fellowship.
Only two last year. Neither is there a parish bar, an idea quite
horrific to Mr Surefaith. Not that his own church hall is
unused—far from it. There is a nightly programme: Sunday:
Sunday Evening Fellowship; Monday: Colts Club (for younger
members); Tuesday: Men's Fellowship; Wednesday: Girl
Guides; Thursday: Women's Fellowship and Bible Study;
Friday: Choir. The church hall is shut on Saturdays since this
is Mr Surefaith's day off. This causes some resentment locally
since the church hall is one of the few possible venues for
wedding receptions, 21st birthday parties and other
community functions. But Mr Surefaith loses no sleep over
this. The church premises are for God's work, for the
proclamation of the gospel message of salvation in Jesus
Christ. And Mr Surefaith is clear that the cause of this

Kingdom is not advanced by a lot of alcohol and disco-dancing.

The congregation at Holy Table are committed, involved and regular (Sunday service averages about 100). Unlike the congregation at St Aloysius, who live in the parish, Holy Table members tend to come from quite far afield. One notices a lot of cars outside the church on Sundays. It seems that perhaps less than half the congregation live in the parish. One splendid advantage of this is that, although the parish and church are quite poor, there are half a dozen church members who give so generously that church maintenance, decorating or the purchase of new hymnals, for example, tends not to be a problem. In his heart Mr Surefaith knows how much pride he feels that the owner of the local textile factory (which employs a lot of people in the parish) is one such benefactor since it was his evangelism with the Holy Spirit that brought this man to Christ at a time when he was suicidal and feeling only life's meaninglessness.

The result of the fellowship being eclectic in this way is a certain distance between the church and the community. Mr Surefaith, for example, tends to visit only his flock. Indeed what else can he realistically do? He works all the hours God sends in just keeping up to date with this.

However, there is a Church of England Primary School in the parish and, as Chairman of the Governors, Mr Surefaith has to be involved here. He sees to it that there is a weekly 'school service' in church. And he regards it as his responsibility to teach scripture to each class weekly. This amounts to two full mornings a week. So his involvement is not *exclusively* with those who attend church.

The strength of the fellowship is the liveliness and power of its faith. There are many stories of healings which have occurred at the monthly healing service. One lady, who had been having chronic trouble with her eyes, and to whom the clinic had offered only drops and ointment, had her sight restored. A man had his cancer put into remission. A girl who had suffered from headaches for years was fully relieved of them. And so on.

The climax of the church's calendar is the annual parish holiday at the 'Centre for Faith and Friendship' near

Blackpool. There are 120 places for this which always go like hot cakes. On this holiday fortnight all age groups come together for a marvellous celebration of the complete Christian family experience. There are short walks and games for the elderly, long hikes and whole day adventures for the young. But in the evenings after supper there are always a couple of hours singing, free prayer, Bible study and sharing in faith. For the regulars it is a school for heaven, a wonderful and joyful expression of all that it means to be a Christian.

Holy Table is particularly active in two other ways. The PCC has a sub-group called the Outreach and Evangelism Committee. Their most ambitious project is to publish a broadsheet six times a year, which volunteers deliver to every home in the parish. This paper always carries the gospel message in summary form so that parishioners at least have a chance to read of the salvation offered them through Christ. Then it has a short review of recent events in church life, a timetable of church activities, details of the entry procedure for the school and other items of interest perhaps submitted by members of the congregation. To show them the church has a brighter side there is often a cartoon of the dirty postcard type, but without the smutty humour. Every autumn there is a more lengthy account of the parish holiday. Before Christmas and Easter the edition emphasizes the times of the main church services.

The other active group is a 'Kind Neighbour' project. The aim is quite simple: to find a way to help a neighbour once a week. This can involve anything from shopping to 'doing the garden' or sitting for a chat over a cup of tea. There are eighteen 'Kind Neighbours' in the scheme at present.

One reason why the Colts are so lively is that Mr and Mrs Surefaith are so very generous with their own home. True, some of the Colts are in any case special friends of their own two teenage daughters, but this is to be expected. Mrs Surefaith in particular sees keeping her house hospitable and open to church members as an important part of her own ministry. Witnessing by the quality of their family life is important to them both. The result is that the vicarage appears to be constantly overrun with boisterous and noisy teenagers crashing up and down the stairs or out into the garden. Members of the Colts Club at least are not likely to tamper with drugs. If only more people in the parish would listen to the saving message of Christ, what natural, God-given human joys could be theirs; what liberation from the death-dealing falsity of the sinful world so evident all around!

The hallmark of the faith at the Church of the Holy Table is its absolute certainty and authority. No one is in any doubt about the inspired truth of the biblical revelation. There *are* doubters at 'Holy Table', but only those on their way in to faith. When insiders begin to doubt they tend not to return. There is little room for those who find themselves unable to agree with Mr Surefaith's teaching. And there is no room at all for questions which challenge or perhaps undermine the faith of the fellowship. The whole point of Christianity is to tell us the answers about life. Questions which obscure the issue come close to blasphemy and cannot be tolerated by Mr Surefaith. Well he knows that some of his members have difficult lives. Some have a tendency towards depression; some show neurotic symptoms. Many, of course, are robust and hearty, but one cannot be too careful in preserving and building up the force of their faith. This is what being a 'shepherd' or pastor means.

Mr Surefaith need not fear. The majority of his congregation will always share a faith like his. They will gladly receive his teaching. Those who do not will be elsewhere.

Saint Jumbo's

The Saint Jumbo's church centre stands on the site of the old vicarage in the next parish along from the Church of the Holy Table. The original Victorian church was pulled down five years ago to make a hostel for persecuted gays and ex-prisoners run by the local authority in conjunction with a charity.

The Vicar, Dave, has a striking and unusual image for a clergyman. He has a punk hair style, slightly dated, and travels round the parish on a powerful motor bike dressed in jeans and appropriate leather. He is a Labour member of the local Council, single, and though himself committed to a vow of chastity, he makes no secret of belonging to 'Proud to be Gay'. In fact it was his personal drive which enabled the redevelopment of the church into a hostel.

Dave hasn't much time for what he calls 'grovelling on your knees religion'. He considers the Church to be culpable in its neglect of social conditions and strongly believes in his political role as an agent of social change. Here are a few lines from one of his recent sermons, (he prefers to call them 'chats') at the Church Centre:

> What's the use of warbling soppy Victorian hymns, making yourself feel all nice and holy when there's no trees for your washing lines outside your own flat kitchens? What's the point of endless prayers and evensongs when the church can't even get it together to house the homeless? The Powers that Be in this country, and I include the government, seem totally and absolutely unconcerned for the lives of real people. And the Church is no better. Millions of pounds it spends on buildings and synods and Bishops' Palaces, but you try to get some money for a project to help handicapped people in this area. Not a chance . . . *Small wonder!*

You can see where Dave's priorities lie. With the oppressed minorities, with people in need and in work for social change. Jesus' message is simple and clear according to Dave. He wants justice for the oppressed, support for the weak and special compassion for the abandoned. Dave feels that professional theology with its abstract books and expensive libraries is a scandal. He once tried to start a group called 'Vicars Against Armchair Academics' but it didn't get off the ground.

Dave's point is that the Church has got an important job to do. It is supposed to bring in the new human community rooted in God's justice. God (Dave likes to call him 'our heavenly care-person') has made his will known and all we have to do is get on with it. Dave says that wrangling about virgin births and resurrected bodies makes him feel sick. The people of God, he says, are a gipsy people called to keep on the move and live in tents. They need to slough off the outmoded bric-a-brac of yesteryear whether it's in the form of stale doctrine or decaying cathedrals.

Organization at St Jumbo's tends to reflect Dave's outlook. Of the twenty-three regular church members sixteen are under forty, left-wing and very socially active. They more or less run the church's groups which are as follows: Housing Action, Women for Women, CND and Jogging Group, Angola Support and Conscientization Group, and The Open Welcome Project. This last is a scheme to share homes with the homeless on a temporary basis. It has caused a good deal of local controversy. Neighbours of the scheme's 'contact people' have twice complained to the Council and to their MP, but to no avail. It is only a modest project, never involving more than about eighteen homeless people. But even so the rumpus has been considerable. One reason is that the 'contact people's' flats are only small so that accommodating, say, four homeless people on their floor does obviously lead to overcrowding. Dave however encourages the scheme precisely as a 'stumbling block', a means of witness to the justice demanded by Jesus. His own accommodation is teeming with marginalized people of mixed ethnic background and with a wide variety of problems. Currently he is in considerable trouble with the church authorities because after he removed his front door as a symbol of welcome no insurance company would continue cover, and not to be insured is against church regulations.

Not all Dave's companions share his somewhat iconoclastic views on worship, and Dave is not so dogmatic as to resist this. Every morning and evening the church centre is open for Zen meditation, yoga, incense-burning and prayer. Dave tends to stay up late at night so that he only rarely appears for the common breakfast of muesli and soya milk with which the morning prayer session finishes.

Sunday worship at St Jumbo's is best described as informal, if not casual. It is as much put together by some of Dave's friends as by himself. They usually begin with a hymn or some taped music. Then there's a reading of some kind from the Bible, or the *Bhagavad Gita* or poetry. Dave insists on reading the gospel appointed for the day. It's a sort of personally imposed reassurance to himself that he's not becoming 'just another social worker'. Then follows a simple Eucharist over which we had better draw a veil lest Dave be in further trouble with the bishop. Suffice it to say that rubrics are not observed and the role allocated to women on some occasions, were it ever to come out, would create uproar.

Before leaving St Jumbo's it is necessary to consider the feelings and attitudes of the parishioners at large to the goings on at the church centre. These are mixed, but one thing is sure: everyone knows who Dave is and he does maintain a flow of friendly chatter with lots of parishioners every day. The result is a favourable groundswell of feeling that Dave is a vicar who's trying to help people. His positive image was reinforced last year when he won the 'Man of the Year' award of the local newspaper for rescuing three old ladies from a flooded basement after the water mains burst. Surprisingly this was the very paper which had dubbed him the 'Pervert Priest' at the time plans for the hostel were going through. One issue ran '"Demolish Church for Dropouts" says Vicar' as its front page headlines and a vicious article on Dave had followed.

Unfortunately St Jumbo's also has numerous enemies. There are those who are scandalized that a priest can be homosexual, those who are offended by his party political involvement, and those who believe he's just not what a priest should be and doesn't do the things a priest should do.

Dave knows he's not perfect and he was mortified by an incident which happened not long after his arrival. An elderly lady, the former sacristan of the church, had committed suicide leaving a letter which held Dave responsible. She wrote:

> Dear God. I know I shouldn't do this but I can't help it. My life's no good any more, just useless. The new priest says you don't care about the church but I do. He's the reason why I've got to do this.

Dave had so much meant to go round and visit her. He had been told she was the mainstay of the church until she'd become ill during the interregnum. But somehow he hadn't found the time. Of course it was kind of his predecessor to come back and take the service for him. It was just before the old church was pulled down. Dave was so upset he doesn't remember much about the service. Only that the church was nearly full, apparently of parishioners. He sometimes wonders who they all were and why they don't still come to church.

The Parish Church

The church along from St Jumbo's is in no danger of demolition. It is the ancient parish church of the area and referred to in most architectural books on important British churches. Unfortunately the medieval stonework is now in an advanced state of decay. The worst affected part is the old bell tower since a major restoration programme in the 1930s already replaced large areas of stonework in the nave and sanctuary. Nevertheless as the roof timbers are also rotting there is currently a restoration appeal for £650,000.

The congregation of 'the Parish Church', as it is always called, are proud of their building. They take their stewardship of it seriously. It is a building with a long history. In the Civil War, for example, it was used as a hiding place for troops; a famous English poet was married there (his signature is kept on display in a beautiful glass cabinet); and the inventor of the alarm clock is buried in the churchyard.

The church is set rather apart from areas of housing, though the population of the parish is 11,000, and includes the most notorious housing estate in the area, the Arcadia Estate, where the riot squad often need to be on hand. Surrounding the church are a motley collection of shops and offices interspersed with some industry. Unfortunately the industry has mostly declined. 70% of local factory space is either empty or up for redevelopment. This is one reason for the very high unemployment in the parish. Shops are closing too, because they are becoming uneconomic since the recent opening of a new hypermarket centre about a mile away. There is concern about this as there is no bus service to the new shopping area. Those without private cars and elderly people are particularly affected. The parish also contains a hospital, a probation office, a police station, and various other statutory and voluntary agencies and offices.

So despite its slight separation of about half a mile from the nearest estate we can say that all human life is there, a stone's throw from the church. The only residential building around is the twelve-bedroomed, eighteenth-century rectory, a listed building, with a high-walled rose garden, fine flowerbeds and lawns. The whole rectory is enclosed by a wall. Even the gates (which lead up the rectory drive) are twenty feet high. You need to be five foot three to reach the stiff iron handle.

The Parish Church is a place of traditions, proudly preserved. Apart from the lovely and historic church with its famous bell tower, there are traditions of good choral singing, a Mayor's service, a lively magazine, a Hospital Volunteer League, brass-rubbing, 'being good with visitors' and bell-ringing. In the mid-nineteenth century a local benefactor endowed money for a choirmaster and the upkeep of good music at the church. This means there is a splendid three-manual pipe organ, and enough money for the post of organist to make the job attractive. At the last vacancy there were forty-eight applications, five with an FRCO, so you can tell the standard is high. There has always been a strong treble line to the choir and the good musical reputation of the church (together with being able to pay the choir) means that the organist has no problem recruiting boys. Some come from as far as ten miles away but are always regular at choir practice. The result is that on Sundays both Mattins and Evensong are accompanied by the most beautiful choral music. A few people in the congregation complain that sometimes the services are more of a concert than an act of worship but in general this is thought to be a price worth paying.

There is a consensus in the congregation that in an uncertain, fallen world the Parish Church has a valuable role in pointing to what is permanent, reliable and sure. 'The Parish Church stands for timeless truths', they say, and they are right. They have had the same churchwardens since 1956, and the order of service has not been tampered with for generations. They are fond of saying, with assurance, '*this* is how we do it at the Parish Church'. One reason why traditions have become time-honoured, is that it is the place where certain people expect certain things to happen. The annual mayoral service, other civic occasions, memorial services, the Remembrance Parade, gatherings of Boys Brigade Battalions and other uniformed organizations, the local school's end of term services—these events naturally take place in the Parish Church.

It is hardly surprising that the PCC's agendas are greatly taken up with maintenance. The Fabric and Restoration

Committee, for example, absorbs the lion's share of the available energy. But there are other committees. Among them is the 'Communications' committee, responsible for the magazine.

Advertising in the magazine is so well organized that it can be printed professionally and still make a profit. The result is the unusual situation where the magazine is given to local shops and offices free of charge for anyone to take. It has been said that 'the only price we pay is that none of the parishioners ever reads the bloody thing', but perhaps this is unkind. Free availability of the magazine is seen as important by the Welcome Committee of the PCC. The group co-ordinates the coming events of church life, organizes brass-rubbing sessions and a rota of stewards to keep the church open at weekends during the summer so that tourists can see the church, the poet's signature and the famous grave. Giving a good welcome is seen as a most important aspect of ministry. It is also important as a source of revenue, something which can't be overlooked when you need £650,000. The Chairman is Lord Faugh who keeps a small city apartment in the parish (having historic family and business connections with the area) and who is a bastion of support to the church. It is out of a concern to keep the welcome open to all that the church magazine never carries features of a political nature. True, PCC meetings take place in the Conservative Club opposite the church, but this is not seen as a 'political' practice; it's just the place the Parish Church PCC has always met.

One church activity which does not revolve around the church itself is the Hospital Volunteer League. These ladies organize a voluntary flower stall at the hospital on two afternoons a week which is much appreciated by visitors. The Rector (Canon Pumpkin, but universally known as 'Rector') has a traditional connection with the hospital (though he is not the official chaplain) and receives an annual income from the Almoners' Company. On certain official occasions (such as the unveiling of the new memorial stained glass window in the hospital chapel) the Rector maintains his role of involvement.

In fact Canon Pumpkin is not able to spend large amounts of time in the parish on account of his dedicated work as a theatre chaplain down in the city centre. He has recently found this work taking up more and more of his time. This is a relief to him. Before his appointment to the theatres he had found his job a bit dull. Visiting was something he didn't find a lot of call for. None of the congregation come from the difficult Arcadia estate so he sees no reason to go there and never did. In any case he has been told it is unsafe. Muggings are common. He had been quite friendly with a few factory executives whom he knew through the local Rotary, but with industry and trade in his area in decline this has not been a lively group lately.

A good deal of his time is inevitably given over to committee work and administration on the restoration appeal. Sunday services take a lot of organizing. Saturdays, too, are busy because the church finds itself in great demand as a place to get married in. The Rector is scrupulous in the observation of legal formalities here. All couples wanting to be married in the Parish Church *must* be on the Electoral Roll in due time so that there is no irregularity. Even so there are some eighty weddings a year. The Rector personally sees each couple for an hour to take them through his *Wedding Guide — handy tips for the marrying couple* which he has had printed. It is important for the Rector to interview the couple as it may be the only occasion on which he meets them informally.

Lastly we must make mention of the bell-ringers. This award-winning group have been on both radio and television. Although they do not actually attend themselves, they are the pride of the church. In 1963 they won a national bell-ringers' award for a perfect peal of Uncle Fred Duples. Their cartoons are imprinted on the Parish Church souvenir coffee mugs. They are the ones who ring out the glory of the ancient Parish Church.

These portraits of St Aloysius, the Holy Table, St Jumbo's and the Parish Church show their pastoral response to be problematic. The Parish Church, for example, manages to ignore completely the notoriously deprived Arcadia estate on its own doorstep. St Jumbo's, despite Dave's radical commitment, is effectively partisan, arbitrarily eclectic, and shows a complete lack of systematic planning and competent administration. Dave's idealism fails to convert itself into realistic and appropriate pastoral goals. Holy Table's response is vitiated by the pastorally disastrous consequences of being more concerned about people's Christianity than their humanity. St Aloysius is unable to marry its important sacramental ministry with many other aspects of pastoral care. The churches portrayed contain men and women of ample sincerity, who are unable to broaden their view so as to encompass a more responsive and collaborative pastoral strategy. As the portraits show, it is all too possible for there to be a serious mis-match between a church and its parish.

Before turning to the whole question of how a church *can* assume the role of pastor in the inner city, I want to focus on the four crucial deficiencies common to each of my caricature parishes and which seriously undermine their ministry.

First, each one expresses the particular outlook and biases of its incumbent. This need not be surprising. Recent research in Chicago has shown how powerfully any congregation is influenced by its minister.[9] So while it is our aim to eradicate an inappropriate dependence on the clergy it must be remembered that as things stand a congregation's vision will be dependent on, and reflect, that of its minister.

Secondly, none of the congregations overcomes its highly self-selecting style. If you are not an obvious candidate to join the 'culture' expressed by each church there is little about their approach to reassure you that you can, nevertheless, be yourself. There is little room for, or encouragement of, individual diversity despite the obvious fact that people are bound to be at different stages in the evolution of their faith, in their emotional maturation and with regard to the energy and insight they possess for giving and receiving. There seems little space to explore the distinctiveness of each person's individuality, especially in that most important area, their seeking after the mystery of the living God.

Thirdly there is no adequate *corporate* Christian formation in any of these congregations. Self-knowledge, deep relationships, a corporate approach to planning for pastoral care, a strategy for the Kingdom—these are not issues to which the riches of Christian tradition seem to be directed. Where a vision of the gospel has been decided upon, it is half-baked. It frequently seems there is no attempt to consider from central principles what it means to be the church and how to proceed in becoming it.

Fourthly, and most glaring of all, the human realities and needs of those beyond the immediate clubbable club of the congregation very easily go unnoticed. Salvation, on any definition, should mean belonging, a healed sense of self, more control, participation in community, acceptance of pent-up and angry feeling, purposefulness, and other signs of hope, social change and liberation. But in each of these parishes the apostolically commissioned agent of salvation, its church, however sincere its members, actually bumbles along fairly satisfactorily without seeing the need to address these fundamental issues with any theological or pastoral rigour.

There is not and never will be some instant salvation to inaugurate a New Age in which the problems of the inner city disappear. But there are resources available to churches through the gospel which can make their contribution distinctive, valuable and hopeful. This is the conviction to be explored in Part Two.

All this can be translated in to other denominations' (NT mention!) language. Few taught have mention).

Notes

1. W. Clebsch and C. Jaeckle, *Pastoral Care in Historical Perspective*, Prentice-Hall 1964, p. 65.
2. Quoted in A. Russell, *The Clerical Profession*, SPCK 1984, p. 113.
3. ibid., p. 115.
4. A. Giddens, *Sociology: A brief but critical introduction*, Macmillan 1986, p. 6.
5. D. Sheppard, *Built as a City*, Hodder and Stoughton 1974, p. 112.
6. ibid., p. 112.
7. *Faith in the City*, pp. 31–33.
8. Derived from DHSS and DE statistics.
9. Referred to by D. Browning (Alexander Campbell Professor of Religion and Psychological Studies at the University of Chicago) in a lecture at the International Pastoral Studies Conference, University of Manchester, July 1986.

PART TWO

The Primary Task of the Inner City Church

Introduction

Each church caricatured in the preceding chapter is making different assumptions about its task. There is nothing new in such a divergence of aims between churches. Throughout its history there have been a variety of models of the Church, leading even during the same period, to strongly contrasting styles of church life. The chantry chapels of the late Middle Ages suggest a church preoccupied with the securing of eternal life for the faithful, and when the Church's task is seen primarily as preparing people for heaven or leading them into mystical communion with God there has always been an emphasis on sacraments, meditative prayer and holy devotions. A church like St Aloysius and All Incense shows that this approach has carried through to the present day. By contrast the Victorian evangelical movement's enthusiasm for mission, with its aims of conversion at home and proselytization abroad, shows a church whose primary emphasis is on the study of Scripture and the dissemination of moral and doctrinal certainties. This is the tradition in which churches like the Holy Table stand. Sometimes the emphasis has been placed on practical acts of charity and service in the world. The example of St Francis typifies this approach and its traces can still be seen in the aims of a church like St Jumbo's with its commitment to community action. As well as their explicitly theological aims, churches have generally had, as sociologists have shown, the implicit function of reinforcing the social and political order of their day. In churches like the Parish Church, which offer a reassuring religious routine and a sense of social and cultural stability, this 'unconscious' role can often predominate.

Each of these churches continues to accept uncritically the appropriateness of its inherited aim. Their failure to examine their situation adequately and plan accordingly prevents their being able to realize their potential as bearers of the gospel of Christ. For lack of clarity and common conviction about the primary task is inevitably debilitating. It leads to confusion, conflict and demoralization. It means that no particular task can be measured against an overall purpose. Without a controlling sense of direction any vaguely worthy task is as valuable as any other. The consequences of such confusion for a UPA church are disastrous. Swamped by human need and in response to the pressures of the demands upon it, such a church swiftly falls into the trap of rushing prematurely into action without having first ordered its priorities. This results in the frustrating sense of having to run hard in order to stand still, or in a flotilla of organizational activities maintained for their own sake. At worst it leads to breakdown or burnout through feeling permanently overwhelmed by the severity of the burden. Someone who starts to attend such a church, say in need of comfort and reassurance after a bereavement, is disabled by an increased sense of obligation instead. In this case the church has failed to notice the actual needs of the newcomer and so failed to respond to them.

It is equally possible for a church to forget that it has a theological purpose: then the symbols and vocabulary of faith such as 'God' and 'salvation' have no functional connection with church activities and float helplessly about them like weightless astronauts. For example, a church may behave as if its primary task was to be a 'supportive community'. Clearly there is a great need for such communities in the inner city and in their various ways pubs, day centres, community halls, lunch clubs and churches respond to this need. But Christian faith concerns more than people's need for support. It addresses itself to our deepest religious needs: our search for God, for example, or our struggle with the contradiction of death in life.

The inner city church should be concerned to *develop the faith* of its parishioners. Certainly it is to receive people as they are and to be a supportive community. Part One has shown the extent to which this will be necessary in a UPA where people may be scarred by the environment, muddled in belief, anxious or angry. But the church's task, by means of the gospel entrusted to it, is to enable these people to grow towards a faith which is truly theirs. This is a faith in God. It is a faith which inspires love of God, love of self and love of neighbour. It is a faith open to the world as it is, yet committed to justice within it. It is a faith which leads to a basic trust in life. It is not a static faith, acquired once for all and thereafter taken for granted. It is a process involving worship, learning, healing and serving as long as life lasts. Therefore an inner city church that is concerned to gain a clear and united sense of its primary task and to do it as well as possible needs to understand what it means to be a *worshipping, learning, healing* and *serving community.* Each chapter in Part Two describes one of these aspects of the overall task and attempts to focus in detail on it and the response it demands from an inner city congregation. But the chapters of course belong together. Only as a whole do they amount to a three-dimensional picture of the primary task of the Church in the inner city.

FOUR

A Worshipping Community

―――――

> It is possible that out of a church *for* the people . . . there
> could come a church *of* the people, a *congregational*
> church . . . In place of a religious ceremony for the people
> each Sunday there can be a feast of the congregation.
>
> Jürgen Moltmann[1]

When I was seven my parents took me to our Anglo-Catholic
parish church for the Maundy Thursday evening liturgy. I got
very excited but cannot now distinguish between enthusiasm
for the service and the promise of fish and chips on the way
home. I do remember coloured vestments, bells, incense,
music and, at the end, a mysterious ceremony called 'the
stripping of the altar'.

Soon after I found myself singing daily Evensong in a
Cathedral choir and for five years as a chorister in Oxford my
life was utterly bound up with the annual cycle of worship
there. In my teens and as a student, even as an ordinand, I
always thought of the church's liturgy as something given.
Something you, as an individual, could learn about and come
to understand. There were the prayer books, lectionaries, and
the feasts and fasts of the liturgical calendar. They were just
there. A person could and should learn about these things in
upbringing, education and by the habit of churchgoing. Once
or twice at University I boldly introduced friends from an
unchurched background to Compline or High Mass assuming
that, with a bit of effort on their part, they would soon be
caught up in what to me was the self-evidently worthwhile
nature of worship as expressed in these time-honoured words
and actions.

I was wrong. The liturgy which through my upbringing
spoke so powerfully to me, generally left my friends

58

untouched. It passed them by. It failed to provide anything they could latch on to.

I found this frustrating. I was convinced that the realities of forgiveness, peace, or blessing, *were* relevant and significant for my friends. But somehow, instead of helping my friends connect with these things the liturgy pushed them further away. Instead of illuminating these truths, the liturgy hid them. Instead of showing Christian faith in an attractive light, the liturgy confused and annoyed. Instead of uniting us, my attempts to share the liturgy with my friends seemed to demonstrate the difference between us.

So as a theological student I spent a lot of time wondering how the Church could rewrite its liturgies to communicate better. I was at the 'bring it to life with guitars' stage, convinced that with a bit of jazzing up in the right places, and by using clear, modern language, the Church's traditional liturgies could break through to people unfamiliar with them. Wrong again. As a curate at the Elephant and Castle I learned the hard way the error of attempts to make the liturgy trendy.

One evening I got into conversation with a young man named Dermot who lived next to the church. It was clear that he was in considerable need. He had just lost his job as a porter at Guys Hospital through persistent lateness on account of drinking. His personal relationships were in tatters, the relationship with his lover broken off. He was in trouble with the police. He had no money. He was on the slippery slope towards the alcoholism and vagrancy I was seeing all round me in the parish. And it suddenly became abundantly clear to me that though Dermot desperately needed the saving experience pointed to in worship, the service I was conscientiously planning for the next morning could do precisely *nothing* to meet Dermot where he was and nor could a thousand refinements of it. I saw then that no amount of tinkering with the churchy end of liturgical expression would reach Dermot. Any hope of Dermot experiencing the grace which for me came through the liturgy would begin by starting with *Dermot's* experience, with *his* feelings and convictions, and discovering what Christian worship meant within them. Otherwise Dermot was never going to make the journey from where he was to an understanding of the Church's concepts and symbols.

That evening I came to appreciate in a very practical way the pastoral futility of a good deal of the liturgy I had been trained to officiate at. Although I did not know what to put in its place I was forced to look at the emptiness of much of the Church's conventional liturgical apparatus when confronted with human need and suffering such as Dermot's. I suspected that the Church needed to make the journey from attachment to its own imagery and ceremony to Dermot's felt experience. Never since then have I thought of liturgy as something whose language the individual has to learn in advance, before being able to participate. During my years as a pastor I have come to learn that good liturgy is always an encounter between Christian tradition and ordinary experience.

Canon Eric James, a leading contributor to *Faith in the City,* has spoken of a similar experience in his own life. His upbringing had led him to music. He was a promising organist with permission to practise on the organ of Southwark Cathedral where he also had lessons. Naturally he enjoyed the beauty of the cathedral's musical tradition and manner of worship, thinking of it as something the church had to offer others. Then he took a job on the wharves of London docks. He met men whose language and whole social world seemed light years away from that of the cathedral. He found himself gazing into a ravine which divided these two worlds. And he was appalled. The Church which meant so much to him had built no bridges of communication between Cathedral-language and dock-talk. The gulf was deep and fixed. And Eric James went forward to ordination, his main desire being to help bridge the gap, to bring together those on either side.

The clear need, then, is to connect worship and ordinary feeling, and for liturgy to transcend the communication gap between different styles of language, barriers of social class and educational background. For this connection to be made, it seems that two conditions need to be met:

— People need to feel they *own* their worship;
— People need to be *full participants* in the worship.

To own your worship you must feel able to come as you are. You must be able to bring your feelings with you. This means that worship must be a safe place to bring anxiety, stress, depression, fear, loneliness, resentment, boredom, illiteracy, diffidence, bitterness, self-pity, grief, shame, anger, madness, guilt, despair, prejudice, hatred, or feelings of oppression. The words of the liturgy must not merely skim the surface of how you feel, leaving you essentially untouched. For example, the prayers of confession can be more than a ritual incantation. A good liturgy is able to confer an *experience of forgiveness.*

To reach people as they are in the inner city, worship must aim to blend tradition and liturgy with the living experience of the worshippers. I do not think it possible to offer a blueprint as to how this is to be achieved. Each congregation's own style of expression in worship is bound to be widely varied. However, the following illustrations taken from an inner city parish in London do show some instances in which worship was brought to life by the participants being able to own what they were doing.

A Mothering Sunday liturgy

According to Church of England rules you must have a licence to preach. But the Bishop had told me that in the inner city we should do whatever seemed right for the Kingdom. So, a month after becoming Vicar, I asked four mothers to give the Mothering Sunday sermon. The theme was to be the relation between the experience of mothering and faith. They were staggered. 'Give the sermon? Us?' 'Yes,' I said, 'Haven't you needed your faith in God since you became a mother?' 'Oh yes,' said Doris, 'when I had my Claire . . .'. At once she started talking. 'That's perfect,' I said with genuine enthusiasm, 'Can you say that on Sunday?' Doris did in fact speak movingly of her experience of God in giving birth. Kate said that it was when she found out that her son David was going to be deaf that she first thought of God, and in different ways each mother was able to say how the experience of mothering had contributed to her faith. They were agreed that it was perhaps their deepest encounter with the mystery of God, as important as anything learned in religious instruction.

That Mothering Sunday sermon deepened the faith of those

who gave it, but it also touched the whole congregation. In particular, people expressed surprise that religion, with its doctrines and creeds, could find room for something as ordinary as being a mother. I was pleased that the sermon was well received, but saddened that the religious expectations of habitual churchgoers should be so removed from their ordinary lives. I subsequently found that considerable imagination was needed to create liturgies around people's deepest personal experiences, but that it was well worth the effort to try. Repeatedly I have found that religion comes alive for people when they are encouraged to see God in experiences like falling in love, having a child, losing a job, or the illness or death of a loved one.

A Memorial Service for Eric

Eric's family felt that his funeral had been impersonal, routine and empty of meaning. It had been conducted by someone who knew neither Eric nor his family and who had therefore used the form of words in the Crematorium funeral book as they stood with no personal references or embellishments. The family were distressed about this and asked if the church could 'do a memorial or something' to help them feel more complete about Eric's funeral and death.

A date was set for the following Saturday morning and it was agreed to hold a preparation in the family home on the previous evening. At the preparation Eric was spoken of and remembered by his family and friends. Each person expressed their grief and mentioned particular feelings of sadness — particular features of Eric which illustrated their grief in losing him. Grief was strongly felt. A good deal of weeping went on. But meanwhile I noted down, in summary, some key points and who had made them. When reassurances had been given amongst the family, by hugging, cups of tea and breaking the grief with humour (which never undermined, blocked or did violence to the grief) attention turned to what it was about Eric that everyone was especially thankful for. Each person was asked to say one or two specific things about him for which they would remain grateful all their lives. This was poignant as one or two people related remarkable incidents in Eric's life unknown to most of the family, while others pointed to qualities in him which not everyone present had appreciated hitherto. On the other hand it also now seemed possible to mention some weaknesses and foibles. There was humour at his expense which went some way to release the group from the lock of grief.

Next the family chose appropriate music, songs on tape and songs to be sung by all. Bible passages were selected and a poem from an anthology. Finally, with help and much to their own surprise, the family prepared a Proper Preface to a eucharistic prayer which was itself a summary of what in Eric gave cause for thanks and praise to God.

Next morning in church there was a sense of expectation. The service took place in an atmosphere of some excitement. In the first parts, 'a Time to be Sad about Eric' and 'a Time to Give Thanks for Eric' each person summarized what they had said the night before but formally, as it were, around the altar—and with accompanying music (on tape), readings, singing, flowers, a celebrant in vestments, and in the church setting.

This was followed by a simple celebration of the Eucharist, including an intensely emotional sharing of the Peace, the Lord's Prayer, Holy Communion, and some final prayers. The liturgy was followed, naturally, by a party. It was felt to be a moving celebration in which, in some mysterious way, Eric and God were both celebrated and made present. It also liberated the family a little from their grief, which they now sensed belonged in the wider context of the glory of God. In addition, the family had experienced a powerfully uniting and even joyful experience at a time when they were feeling fragmented and, as individuals, isolated by grief.

This worship married Christian liturgical tradition with the actual feelings of a particular set of people in a particular time and place. On the one hand there was Christ made known again in the breaking of bread and the offering of praise and thanksgiving to God, after repentence; on the other there were three generations of a grieving family with little experience of church life but able, on this occasion, to participate in worship of God with strong feelings of personal involvement.

The Need for Creative imagination in funerals.

The Baptism, Confirmation and Funeral of John

John, aged forty, was found to have cancer secondaries in his stomach and had only a few weeks to live. A short time before, in the first shock of learning the nature of his illness John and his family had begun a relationship with their parish church and had been coming on Sundays. John made friends quickly. He was a warm and attractive person and something of an extrovert (a talented singer and entertainer) with an easy and obviously genuine interest in others.

Before his illness John had been an enthusiastic sportsman. He had the build and strength of a rugby forward. As his massive weight loss occurred and his energy began to wane he and the family asked if there could be a service in church for him. They wanted to offer God their situation and ask for healing, and John himself wanted to be baptized. The family knew the seriousness of John's illness and felt God would be able to meet them in their plight, although wisely they did not attempt to prescribe how.

The family, with my help, prepared the shape of the service and chose suitable readings. After the rite of baptism John sang 'I'll walk with God from this day on.' It was deeply moving. Prayers followed and then the laying on of hands. First family, then friends and anyone from the congregation took part in this. They said prayers over John, and the family remained with him to hold and be present with him as others came up to lay on hands and to pray. John himself prayed that he would find God in what he was undergoing.

The striking thing about the service was the exceptional sense of fellowship it engendered. People seemed somehow united with John through the liturgy. It conferred a sense of peace and inner strength on John, his family and, it seemed, all who took part. John's situation and suffering did not prevent the growth of a love in which people gave and received from each other. It was that rare occasion when participants feel moved and softened by a sense of the surrounding presence of God. A fortnight later the Bishop came to confirm both John and his wife in a second service at which they both read and he again sang.

John remained at peace during the last weeks of his life. His final prayers were all thanksgiving and intercession for others. At his funeral his wife and four children gathered round the altar with the celebrants so as to surround John's coffin and face the rest of the congregation. Together they joined in part of a eucharistic prayer written for the occasion, and shared communion. They were too overwhelmed by grief to be able to disentangle feelings, faith and despair. But for many in the congregation it was a liturgy in which faith found itself and God became known in a new way.

Mary, John's wife, found her family extended by her involvement with the church. Some of her healing was certainly brought about as a result of the new friendships she made. But Mary has said that what she received from the church at that time went beyond friendship and must include the experience of God she recognized in the church's *worship*. Mary's discovery points to the intimate link between the quality of a congregation's worship and the quality of its pastoral care. The gospel's latent power of healing can be celebrated, made explicit and enjoyed in Christian worship, and indeed everything about Christian community is rooted in worship since its very existence is a response to God. This is what makes the Church's care distinctive in the inner city or elsewhere. It is the belief that the ultimate empowering force behind the universe is God's love, 'the love which moves the sun and the stars', as Dante put it, which sets Christian pastoral care apart from the other therapies offered by secular humanism. But it is in *worship* that this belief is celebrated in common. From this it follows that, from the viewpoint of pastoral care, there is something of the highest importance at stake in whether or not a congregation's worship realizes the latent healing power that lively worship offers.

Preparing worship together

The examples I have given so far each started with a strongly felt experience in the lives of particular individuals and described how an act of worship could be built out of that experience. But it is perhaps not surprising that the peak life events of birth, marriage and death, events which are central to all social and religious ritual, should lend themselves to this approach. It is much more problematic to achieve effective and compelling Sunday worship where the themes and readings are prescribed by the lectionary, and where there may often be, or appear to be, no intense or deeply felt communal experience round which a liturgical form can coalesce. How can worship connect with ordinary living and touch personal needs when so much of its content is given, prepackaged and ready to use, in the ASB? This is the key question. Most inner city people simply are not accustomed to liturgical worship and it is difficult for those who have been preparing these words for years to understand that they can seem alien and off-putting. I am moved by the Collect for Purity every time I say it. Yet from the viewpoint of someone like Dermot the liturgical jargon of Rite A blocks out its meaning. There was hardly anything he needed more than a sense of being forgiven. And he was quite ready to say he was sorry for what he felt was wrong in his life. But for him the pronouncement 'God gave his only Son Jesus Christ to save us from our sins, to be our advocate in heaven, and to bring us to eternal life', even delivered in one's best liturgical accents, cannot meet his need because its language does not connect with the language of his need.

It can come as a shock to inner city clergy when they discover how much of what they take for granted is in fact a stumbling block even to regular members of the congregation. Although for years they may continue meekly to mouth the words set before them people may say, when asked, that they think the confession is hypocrisy, the gloria gibberish (not to mention the creed) and much of the Eucharist a magical rite more to the glory of the priest than God.

Some styles of worship assume that the liturgy will meet people's needs simply by providing an ambience suitable for an encounter with the mystery of God: candles flickering in the Lady Chapel, the white lamp of the reserved sacrament, ikons and statues and coloured seasonal fittings may combine with the scent of incense to encourage a mood of prayer and a sense of the numinous, to raise up the congregation from the ordinariness of the workaday world. But this cannot replace the need for people to make more explicit connections between worship and their own experience. Neither can it be an adequate substitute to simply ignore whatever in Christian tradition is difficult or distasteful, as at St Jumbo's. Christians

believe that God makes himself known in worship, which
requires worshippers to draw on *all* that is included in the
story of God's revelation to his people, n ɔt just those parts of
the story they happen to like. If liturgy is reduced to being a
vehicle of self-expression it cannot convey what lies at the
heart of worship: the transcendent mystery of God.

Atmosphere is of course important and, for the necessary
connections to be made, it must be an atmosphere of welcome.
Newcomers need to be helped to feel they will be accepted as
they are and that the worship is addressed to them as they
are. This requires more than a bland announcement that the
service begins on page 119 and that everyone is invited
afterwards for tea. A convincing welcome then needs to be
endorsed by the openness of attitudes in the congregation
and by the general feel of things. The church interior, for
example, will already have sent out a powerful signal to the
newcomer. Churches which display a single poster, for the
Diocesan Hassock-Making Guild, and put out a single
collecting box for the church flowers, feel introverted and
ecclesiastical. Churches awash with boldly-coloured children's
art displays, posters for Christian Aid and the Movement for
the Ordination of Women, photographs of church office-
holders or parish outings—or which have a well-stocked
bookstall, an intercessions book, a suggestions box, and
show evidence of action and involvement in the local
community—inevitably feel more alive, more fun and more
likely to mean what is said in the welcome. In an authentic
worshipping community there is an almost tangible sense of
liberation from narrow stereotyped views and expectations.
Instead there is an atmosphere of exploration and discovery,
a felt respect for the different faith of others. There is the
quiet assumption that when each person prays in their own
way, the faith of the whole congregation is enhanced. The
priority of connecting liturgy to the personal experience of the
individual should not be mistaken for an attempt to privatize
the worship. It is essential for worship to be meaningful to
each person privately but absolutely wrong ever to claim that
Christian worship is capable of only private meaning. From
the time Moses asked Pharoah to let the Hebrews go to
worship their God in the desert for a day or two, worship of
our God has been a corporate affair. Its meaning cannot be

privatized. Christian worship has something of the
community atmosphere of the upper room at Pentecost about
it. It is inseparable from proclamation of, and gathering to
celebrate, God's Kingdom. The Peace during the Sunday
Eucharist, for example, is often something of a climax in a
UPA church. It can be a poignant gesture of reconciliation
after a row, a time to hug the bereaved, to greet unfamiliar
people or a time for a moment of humour with a friend.
Barchester congregations, who squirm at the very thought of
such an unbuttoned interruption of Divine Service, are sadly
deprived of this capacity to share human warmth, and inner
city churches here have an advantage over them in being able
to express their corporateness with less inhibition.

The manner and lead of the celebrant is obviously
important in establishing the mood and vitality of the liturgy.
Clerical sing-song or prayers recited parrot-fashion, for
example, instantly destroy it. The sensitive addition of free
prayer or leaving a space for silence can assist it. For example,
in the opening penitential rite the celebrant can explicitly
acknowledge that people are bringing their needs to church
and invite members of the congregation to recollect their
feelings—whatever they are—and use them as a basis for
their worship. Such an introduction can enable people to tune
in to their *whole* selves and to the liturgy itself. But a decisive
way forward to achieve the sought-for connections between
liturgy and experience is for the congregation to prepare its
own Sunday Eucharist. The sense of involvement that this
confers generates new life like spring after winter. You need
only participate in this process once for there to be a kindling
effect with enduring results. I have found that for a
congregation to do this, for it to experience owning its
worship, is a watershed. It results in the discovery of fresh
meaning, powerful fellowship and renewed worship of God
as the source of grace.

Any group of any age can participate in preparing the
worship or, at a 'parish weekend', for example, the whole
congregation can do it. Clearly it is important to plan how the
preparation is going to be done. People will need space at the
start to say how they feel at the prospect of preparing worship,
especially if it is not something they have done before. It will
no doubt be a relief to them to discover that others feel as

diffident and hesitant as they do. If more than a small number
of people are involved it will be practical to share the task by
dividing into small groups. Depending on the number of
people available groups might be given the choice of preparing
either the penitential rite, the ministry of the Word, the
intercessions or the eucharistic prayer, being responsible for
co-ordination or choosing the music.

Those who opt to prepare the *ministry of the Word* face the
task of imaginatively communicating the theme of the day, as
illustrated in the readings. They may use drama, movement,
drawing, music or spoken explanation. They will of course
have to study the readings and will no doubt wish to draw on
what they themselves have learned while doing the
preparation. They do not need to present a common view.
Differences can reinforce the vitality of the presentation as
long as it is cogent, carefully rehearsed and sufficiently short.
Those preparing *the intercessions* need to keep in touch with
any other group in order to blend their themes, feelings and
hopes into the prayers and offer up the action or change of
heart which might arise from the service. They also need to
be flexible: Someone may ask for the laying on of hands.
People may want time to contribute their own biddings. A
long silence may seem appropriate or, on the contrary, a
speedy ending if, for example, the chorus of wailing infants is
becoming too painful. However well they prepare, the
intercessions group need to read the signals coming from the
congregation at the time. The group preparing the *eucharistic
prayer* should combine its traditional shape and content
(preface, *epiclesis,* institution narrative, *anamnesis* and
doxology) with the freshness of what this particular worship
has celebrated. Since the eucharistic prayer is central in
maintaining Christian continuity it must be in this sense
conservative and theologically well-earthed. But this doesn't
mean sticking punctiliously to some specified form of words.
The preface, for example, can succinctly incorporate images
or phrases from what has gone before, summarizing, but in a
eucharistic context. In this way it becomes a thanksgiving in
which *today's* themes and intentions can be built onto the
recital of the great acts of God in the history of faith—a sign
of this congregation's being one with the pilgrim people of
God whose story they have just read in the Bible.

The corporate preparation of worship will result in more than lively liturgy on Sundays, it will nurture the prayer of the congregation. An almost imperceptible growth of spiritual confidence seems to be gained by belonging to a fellowship in which you experience the faltering attempts of other people just like you trying to say their prayers. Shared prayer assists in learning to pray. And shared preparation of Sunday worship enhances the church's response to liturgical celebration in general so that a youth group, a group of women, or elderly or unemployed people might prepare and lead a service where this would have been unthinkable before. Similarly the events and seasons of the calendar such as Advent, Christmas, even Harvest Festival, can find a significance they lacked while the church's liturgy remained over against the ordinary experience of people rather than in conversation with it. But it is during Lent, Holy Week and Easter that the liturgical year provides the greatest opportunity to interiorize what it means to be a Christian. And by preparing for Holy Week and Easter as a congregation inner city people can come to experience how the climax of the Christian story—the suffering, death and resurrection of Christ—connects with their own story.

One way to achieve this connection is by using one's imagination. Each member of a group might be asked to identify with one person involved in the passion drama: Peter, for example, or Judas or Mary Magdalene. After time for preparation each person can be asked to describe the story as they have experienced it in the role of their chosen character. Exercises like this can bring the story of Christ's Passion alive. But there is also the need for people to connect their story with the Easter symbolism of new life through death. In Tottenham one year we attempted to do this by organizing such a wide variety of Lenten activities that everyone would (we hoped) find a suitable means of preparing for Easter. There was dancing, painting, handicrafts, singing and making an Easter garden in the churchyard as well as prayer and discussion groups. Each activity was designed to help prepare for Easter. The dancers, for example, prepared a dance to convey in movement the passion and resurrection of Christ which they danced during the Easter services.

The liturgical drama of Holy Week speaks loud in a UPA because it is something done rather than conceptualized. Provided that inner city people participate fully in it and feel they own it, their worship can be lifted out of imprisonment in prayer book texts and kissed into life.

Notes

1. J. Moltmann, *The Open Church*, SCM 1978, pp. 115, 124.

FIVE

A Learning Community

Be renewed in the spirit of your minds, and put on the
new nature, created after the likeness of God.

Ephesians 4.23, 24.

A Christian view of learning

The Chief Rabbi, Lord Jakobovits, has offered a Jewish view
on *Faith in the City*. In it he suggested some alternative
approaches derived from Jewish teachings and experience.
He described how the Eastern European Jewish immigrants
of the 1880s achieved their emancipation from the ghettos
during the century that followed and asked what lessons
could be learned from their success. Quoting from an address
he had given in New York in 1966 he wrote:

> How did *we* break out of our ghettos and enter the
> mainstream of society and its privileges? How did *we*
> secure our emancipation and civil rights? Certainly not by
> riots and demonstrations, by violence and protest-marches,
> or by preaching 'Jewish power' or even non-violence. Above
> all, we worked on ourselves, not on others. We gave a
> better education to our children than anybody else had. We
> hallowed our home life. We channelled the ambition of our
> youngsters to academic excellence, not flashy cars. We
> rooted out crime and indolence from our midst, by making
> every Jew feel responsible for the fate of all Jews.[1]

Lord Jakobivits wanted to offer the same advice to West
Indians in Brixton in 1986 that he had given to New York
blacks in 1966: they should give two or three hours extra
schooling every day to their children like the Jews in the
ghettos had done, and use education as an escape route out of
inner city deprivation and into middle class equality. It is

72

what
twit?

possible to react angrily to the Chief Rabbi's critique of *Faith in the City* by arguing that it does not take adequate account of racism, ethnic educational disadvantage and, in general, the many factors which destroy morale in urban priority areas. The intractability of inner city problems stems from the inhibited sense of self, the diffidence and resultant educational apathy which cruelly paralyzes precisely that spirit of resilience, of 'get up and go', needed for liberation from the ghetto. And the highest trump card held by the Jewish community, solidarity in family life, is the one most lacking in the present climate of increasing family breakdown, single-parent families and child abuse.

Education Authorities in inner cities are aware of the vital links between schooling, family life and environment. Many have taken imaginative initiatives to make the necessary connections. Community schools have been developed and parental involvement increased. And inner cities abound in alternative educational projects, self-help groups and community learning enterprises from drama workshops to Chinese massage. But from the viewpoint of *Faith in the City* or of a book concerned with pastoral care in urban priority areas, the Chief Rabbi's advice is of little help. While he portrays the Jewish experience as the success of one close-knit ethnic group in breaking out of the ghetto, the churches' concern is for whoever has to take their place in that same ghetto. Our aim is to understand and change the structures which keep somebody at the bottom of the pile, and with the pastoral care of those who will always find themselves in that situation whilst such structures remain. The Chief Rabbi advocates better schooling as the best means for the fittest to fight their way out of the ghetto. But pastoral care in a UPA will need to draw from a much broader sense of learning than mere schooling. The idea of learning, in the sense we shall need to use it, goes to the very heart of Christian faith and becomes a theme of far-reaching pastoral implications.

The Christian understanding of learning stems from the core of what we believe about ourselves as creatures of God. In Genesis the creation myth captures the insight that the restless searching of men and women for new ideas and discovery is an indispensable part of their humanity. This capacity to learn is a universal human inheritance, not a *there we go again.*

question of schooling an elite. In a lecture on man the late Sydney Evans suggested that the Fall story points to the essence of the distinctively Christian understanding of learning as human growth. Whereas ideologies like Marxism blame human nature for such critical problems as poverty and structures of injustice, and religions like Buddhism dismiss such problems as illusions, Christianity sees these human contradictions as the *raw material of growth:* they must be faced, and worked through. In that very learning process we make our response to the redeeming love of God.

Does it —ically

The Christian view of learning goes beyond the idea of formal education to include all that is involved in human growth. St Paul clearly thinks of the Church as growing through learning. In Colossians he calls Christ 'the Head, from whom the whole body nourished and knit together through its joints and ligaments, grows with a growth that is from God' (Col. 2.19). He speaks of the Church as those who are 'to be conformed to the image of his Son' (Rom. 8.29). In exhorting the Galatians he refers to his 'travail until Christ be formed in you' (Gal. 4.19). His prayer in Ephesians is nothing if not an appeal for a learning church:

> That you being rooted and grounded in love, may have power to comprehend with all the saints what is the breadth and length and height and depth, and to know the love of Christ which surpasses knowledge, that you may be filled with the fullness of God. (Eph. 3.15—19)

And in the next chapter Paul describes his vision of the Church as growing to a full maturity in Christ so that:

> Speaking the truth in love, we are to grow up in every way into him who is the head, into Christ, from whom the whole body . . . when each part is working properly, makes bodily growth and upbuilds itself in love. (Eph. 4.12—16)

It is not only St Paul who describes a learning Church. The Gospels also presuppose the need for change, learning and human growth. The story of the twelve disciples that begins with their call by Jesus, is the story of a community who, with much stumbling and failure, gradually learn to see and to live in the light of what Jesus has tried to teach them and be for them. According to St Matthew the crowds were 'astonished at his teaching' (Matt. 7.28), and one has only to glance at the Beatitudes to see why. They are not teachings which can be assimilated by intellectual study—they require a lifetime of learning in a learning community.

In the Christian tradition learning is all that is involved in growing towards maturity in Christ. While it is true that at the centre of Christian faith lies the paradox that one must die to self in order to live, with its consequence of taking up the cross and following Christ, it is not true that this implies a closed attitude to learning. On the contrary, maturity in Christ implies a self-knowledge and a knowledge of God that has been and is still being learned. Self-giving is far from mindless self-surrender. Self-giving is possible only through a personality; it cannot substitute for personality. The parable of the talents invites us to realize potential, not to bury it. Once learning is understood as 'learning to be in Christ', it is clear that much is at stake in whether or not a UPA church actually is a learning community. The gospel of Christ potentially meets the deepest needs and addresses itself to the most pressing human problems of inner city people. To people who lack identity and are full of guilt, who feel alienated, unwanted and purposeless, it offers a relationship with God that roots the whole of life in a love from which there can be no separation (Rom. 8.38). And through the Church the gospel potentially offers the friendship of the community who share this experience of divine love and seek to live in response to it; fellowship, in other words, in a community whose values are love, forgiveness, welcome and hope, rooted in worship. The power of the gospel is that the mystery of 'Christ in you, the hope of glory' (Col. 1.27) can be made manifest now in face-to-face relationships. This is achieved whenever a church collaborates with the surprising love of God to work through the contradictions of inner city life in defiant response to its damaged environment and circumstances. But this gospel and these transforming values remain frozen as potential until they are *learned*, which is why a church must be, or become, a learning community.

What Christians have to learn about does not sound much if you say it fast: self, others, God and the world they live in. Christians do not learn only for the sake of learning (enjoyable though some learning can be). They learn because they want

to be effective in building the Kingdom. It may or may not be
pleasurable for me to learn something new about myself but I
can hardly learn to love others effectively if I am closed to
learning about my feelings or why I react as I do. Similarly,
other people may or may not fascinate me but I can hardly
learn to love them if I am closed to learning how they feel. In
either case, I need to learn where I am blind, prejudiced or
defensive, and how I can better perceive the needs (perhaps
unspoken) of those around me. Christians aspire to learn
about God in the very act of calling themselves Christian.
The first commandment, to 'Love the Lord your God with all
your heart, with all your soul, and with all your mind' (Matt.
22.37), is presumably one which requires your whole life to
obey. All Christian prayer belongs within the Christian school
of prayer. All worship and prayer are learned. God does not
reveal himself automatically like a teleprinter. And Christians
learn about the world in general and their local situation in
particular so that they can work appropriately for justice and
peace, assess needs and use their resources to meet them and
proclaim the gospel in terms that are relevant and convincing.
Neither pastoral care nor evangelism can be planned without
learning about the setting in which it is supposed to be taking
place.

Since practically everything in Christianity involves
learning, it is a horrible irony that in practice the Church so
often fails to live up to its calling, and that many churches
appear to have stopped learning in this broadest sense at all.
Some church congregations leave you with the distinct
impression that Christianity does not particularly have
anything to do with learning or growing. And the pointed
question which has to be asked is this: If learning to be in
Christ is such an integral part of Christian living, how come
so many churches seem so content to stand still? This question
is a forceful challenge since it is sadly clear that many people
have belonged to churches for years without learning much at
all. Such people might not dream of accepting that they
should have moved on. If what matters most to you about
belonging to St Aloysius is being in charge of the tea rota why
bother to learn something new about the Bible? If you've
always disliked Florrie Grundles and are famous for it in
church life why worry further about the Gospels' teaching

on forgiveness? A situation can develop in which churchgoing
is felt to be satisfactory and worthwhile even though learning
has stopped. Worse, it is possible for the habit of churchgoing
to become a palliative which actually *prevents* learning in one
or more of a variety of ways.

Blocks to learning

The forces which get in the way of religious learning tend to
result from either our need for *security,* which can inhibit our
desire to learn, or our *fears,* which can easily lead us to feel
threatened. Since both insecurity and fear are endemic
problems of the inner city these blocks to learning need to be
understood and removed if congregations are to become
learning communities.

1. *The Hope for Haven*

Many members of St Aloysius and All Incense, the Holy
Table, St Jumbo's and the Parish Church find the problems
and demands of Monday to Friday a hard grind. What they
want at weekends is an escape from the turmoil—a retreat to
the bosom of the family and the peace of mind they find from
going to church. But in so far as Fr Halo, Mr Surefaith, Dave
and Canon Pumpkin collude with their congregations' bid to
remain in perpetual religious childhood and are willing to let
them keep up the myth of religion as a haven there is a price
to be paid: they must stop learning. For example, although
there has been a revolution in theology, biblical studies and
religious culture, although Bultmann, Bonhoeffer and John
Robinson have lived and died, they must be sure to take no
notice. When the Bishop of Durham raises his critical
questions they must not listen. Only then can their peace of
mind remain undisturbed. A variation on this theme is the
tribal approach to religion, seen to some extent in Chapter
Three's presentation of both the Church of St Paul and the
Holy Table and St Aloysius and All Incense. In these churches
a reassuring transmission of tribal solidarity is what is all-
important. Liturgical language must not be tampered with
and ritual must not be changed, or the 'tribal identity' could
not be passed on. Obviously these congregations have to

remain passive and too much new learning is out of the question. The authority of the tradition is what matters. These congregations are, from a religious point of view, entirely bound to their past. They use the biblical tradition in order to stay in the ancient world from which they came rather than to grow towards the new and as yet undiscovered world to which the Bible might point.

The opposite of this approach, seen in the liturgy at St Jumbo's and in a more general context at the Parish Church, is the *autonomous-individual* approach in which worship or the beliefs of religion are seen as an entirely private affair. Since learning usually involves bringing people together to *share* their beliefs (a ghastly prospect to the privatizer-brigade) you can be sure such a congregation will go all out to resist learning. Interestingly the Parish Church manages to combine the contradictory features of both the tribal and autonomous-individual approaches on account of its need for both private personal religion *and* social solidarity. All these features stem from the hope for haven.

2.   *The Flight from Fear*

Fear does for learning what a head-on wind does for a cyclist. And fear is aroused whenever faith is threatened. Mr Surefaith cannot cope with those who 'doubt' in his congregation because his own faith expresses what he values about himself. Consequently if someone in his church challenges his faith he feels it is a challenge to his 'self': loss of faith to him means loss of self. He resists facing up to his own doubts from a fear of being disloyal to what he has come to value about himself. And where he does begin to feel doubt he is particularly fearful of learning more about it in case what he discovers leads to even more doubt. Mr Surefaith and the congregation at Holy Table are especially vulnerable to threat in this way since their religion is such a tightly coded and exclusive pattern of belief 'guaranteed' by an unquestioned biblical authority. Father Halo's theological conservatism, exemplified by his passionate resistance to the ordination of women, is explained by the presence in him of the same kind of fear. He believes that what he calls 'the historic tradition' must be handed down unchanged because the risk of unsettling the faith which is the ground of his life might prove too painful. Any disturbance of his most deeply held assumptions might threaten his whole identity.

The more vulnerable members of churches like St Aloysius and Holy Table try to fly from the fear involved in learning by various techniques which, alas, turn out to be false trails failing to take them out of the wilderness. Some inner city dwellers are particularly prone to follow such trails, for they have led lives in which they have too often been found wrong or been made to feel guilty or unacceptable. As a result they are willing to follow the Yellow Brick Road of 'belief' without question. They willingly take the path of *blind acceptance* because it appears to lead away from confusion, since God's truth is indisputably known, and away from guilt, because God's will can unequivocally be done.

Another technique to avoid fear is to *shut out religion* altogether. The congregation at the Parish Church are good at this, making church life revolve around choir, nice flowers and the bell-ringing. The aim is to distract attention away from beliefs at all costs. A variation on this, used with advantage at St Jumbo's, is to be so excessively *vague about belief* that no one could possibly be threatened because nothing is particularly being demanded by way of belief in the first place. The method preferred by some at St Aloysius is to be so *pietistically obsessed* with religious observances like going to Mass and Benediction that they do not notice their doubts; and since Fr Halo can be so totally trusted to know what matters it is far more comfortable to accept reassurance from him than discover the meaning of religion for themselves.

Unfortunately there is neither security nor much relief from fear in burying your head in the sand, only ignorance of reality. Doubt creeps back or boredom sets in. Sooner or later these tricks lead to exhaustion. They fail to give the desired reassurance. The way of unlearning does not work and no salvation lies along it.

Enabling learning

In the light of the Christian acceptance of Jesus Christ as 'the Way, the Truth and the Life' (John 14.6), as the one who came that we 'might have life and have it to the full' (John 10.10)—and whose Spirit will lead us 'into all truth' (John 16.13)—it is only to be expected that palliative manoeuvres will fail to satisfy human beings. Church congregations are called precisely 'to grow up in every way . . . into Christ' (Eph. 4.12). And if God is the God we believe he is, a God who makes himself known, he will do just that and go on doing so. He will not stop communicating himself to his creatures because in our attempt to grow and learn we have new ideas, even if some of them are bad. This is why we can be completely open to challenging critical questions and new thinking. We are not obliged to agree but we should be able to face what they say. Even 'traditional' ideas and symbols or biblical parables, myths and sagas, psalms and prophetic writings are *resources for further growth* as human beings. The Bible is not a *Manifesto of Right Belief* issued by the Thought Police of the Ministry of Christian Truth.

In a UPA this vocation to 'grow up into Christ' could hardly be more needed. The way to discover identity, grow in confidence, calm fear and feel more secure, is to belong to a learning community. Belonging and learning go together. One cannot grow up into Christ by Correspondence Course; Christian nurture cannot take place in that way. Just as the infant needs a parent to hold and 'contain' it while it learns to manage anxieties and internalize enough safety to continue emotional development, so Christians need a holding environment or community to sponsor the development of their faith. Growth in faith is an aspect of human development. They go together or not at all. And since faith is in part an expression of a person's self-image and the view of the world they have developed over their whole life, it is inevitable that deep faith will from time to time become deep doubt. For it is an unusual person who is not occasionally prone to self-doubt. Jesus was himself tempted in the wilderness, found himself in agony at Gethsemane and cried out in dereliction from the cross. Those who, like James Fowler,[2] have made a particular study of faith development in relation to human growth, make it clear that 'doubt is part of the life of faith, for the successive images of the life of faith destroy their predecessors.'[3] Robert Kegan,[4] another developmentalist, has also shown the importance of religious doubt

as an essential prelude to each movement through the stages
of faith's evolution. As in worship, so in learning, exploration
becomes more desirable, more attractive than stagnation,
when it touches on a person's own story.

Someone known to me, we'll call her Elizabeth, went to a
church which organized discussion groups every Lent. She
had always gone to these, thinking of them as a kind of adult
Sunday School which she ought to attend because it was
good for her like cod liver oil. She was always bored because,
although she couldn't see it, her churchgoing and her faith
were a crutch she leant on as a defence against the far worse
anxiety of being alone in her flat. During one of these meetings
another woman in the group began to talk about her own
loneliness, her sense of isolation from other people and her
unhappy childhood as a result of which she felt more hate
than love for God. Elizabeth found herself crying. This was
her story too and she recognized it and began to face up to it
for the first time. From then on Elizabeth's involvement in
the church felt more real. She went to see the curate saying
that she wanted to learn how to pray. He suggested that she
wrote down on a piece of paper all the images of God and
feelings about God she could remember from the time of her
childhood onwards. At first she was reluctant to do this as
she immediately felt the pain and fearfulness of some of these
memories. Gradually she began to see that she was still
carrying with her a paralyzing relationship with God inherited
from her childhood, and that this God was a tyrant and not
the God seen in the Jesus of the Gospels. Her adult religious
learning had begun.

The story of Elizabeth shows that churches do not have to
abandon the responsibility to be learning communities in
order to take seriously a person's hurt past which has resulted
in a fear of or a resistance to learning. On the contrary it is
only when religious defences are understood and responded
to sensitively that learning can begin. A learning congregation
enables each of its members somehow to review their spiritual
life story and accepts each story as equally valid, just as it
acknowledges that everyone equally is a daily beginner in
learning about God.

To promote a learning congregation it is clearly necessary
to plan suitable structures in church life for learning to take

place. The traditional pattern of weekly worship, Parochial Church Councils, social functions, fund-raising events and various kinds of community campaigns is totally inadequate by itself. New structures for learning, in small groups for example, must be invented to supplement it. Obviously such structures must fit in with the lives of busy and committed people who may well feel they do not have much time to give directly to church activity, and who are concerned that the time they do have should be used for effective practical action rather than in sitting about doing something nebulous called 'learning'. But I believe it is time to establish a pattern of church life wherein most people, at least for some of the year, are prepared to give an hour and a half a week beyond Sunday worship for a church event in which, whatever else its practical purpose may be, learning takes place. My experience confirms that this hope is realistic, though it may take some years to achieve. Most churches by now at least have Lent Courses or some kind of house-group. But if a church has *not* yet developed a thirst for learning it is obvious that an ambitious educational programme cannot be ushered in overnight. A sermon here, a workshop there, a modest pilot scheme of four group sessions with a piece in the magazine, are sufficient as a start. We have seen how deep resistance to religious learning can be and it follows that over-zealous attempts at a sort of mini cultural revolution will prove counterproductive. The most defensive people feel alienated and leave. Others will feel an inflated excitement based on false expectations irresponsibly aroused, only to find disappointment in what actually happens.

Fostering a learning atmosphere is a subtle business, since, as in worship, the spirit of a particular church is conveyed more by the quality of relationships between members—the feel in the congregation—than by the curriculum detailed on the first page of the parish magazine. Impressive structures for learning, a timetable jammed with hearty house-groups, may turn out to conceal a highly defensive attitude to learning. Structures aren't everything. It's possible that a congregation making comparatively little use of small groups *could* be very open to learning. Their worship, fellowship and response to the wider community might prove this. But there is considerable room for deception. A parish with no educational programme, no small groups, study weekends, retreats or learning courses is most unlikely to feel like a parish foraging after truth. And if this is so can they be surprised if their pastoral response to the wider community is as dead as the dodo?

The example set by the clergy will be extremely influential in whether or not the congregation are enabled to grow. If the clergy model an attitude of learning, openness and vulnerability the congregation will learn to be learners just by belonging. They will make the discovery that prayer and learning, or seeking the Kingdom and learning, belong together. Thus the God they have perhaps hitherto only called upon to help them out in a crisis, is slowly able to become the God who is calling them to help in his creative and loving purpose.

Learning and growth in Christ are central to pastoral care in UPAs because without nurture there is no framework upon which to connect people's hurt and the resources of faith. The late Professor R. C. P. Hanson of Manchester University has questioned whether any other power than the gospel *can* meet the deepest needs of people in our culture. Asking what beliefs lie behind the popular media he answers: 'an ill-assorted collection of principles . . . a kind of individualistic, positivist, tolerant hedonism'. And he concludes: 'It is inconceivable that this philosophy could infuse or sustain a civilization for more than a very short time.'[5] He suggests that in Christianity alone there might be the hope of a new post-Marxist, or even non-Marxist, civilization. This is a hope which those who feel trapped for ever in our inner cities need to hold on to.

Notes

1. *From Doom to Hope: A Jewish View on Faith in the City.* Office of the Chief Rabbi 1986, p. 5.
2. J. W. Fowler, *Stages of Faith: The Psychology of Human Development and the Quest for Meaning,* New York, Harper and Row 1981.
3. J. M. Hull, *What Prevents Christian Adults from Learning?,* SCM 1985, p. 186.

4. R. Kegan, *The Evolving Self: Problem and Process in Human Development,* Harvard University Press 1982.
5. These quotations are from Hanson's article in *The Times,* 10 September 1983. For an excellent exposition of the power of Christian theology to address an inner city situation see L. Green, *Power to the Powerless,* Marshall Pickering 1987.

SIX

A Healing Community

Christian community is a gift of God which we cannot claim . . . It is not an ideal which we must realize; it is rather a reality created by God in Christ in which we may participate . . . it is a spiritual and not a psychic reality.
Dietrich Bonhoeffer.[1]

The primary task of an inner city church is to help match God's gifts in the gospel to the needs of the people who live there. Healing is of course a central theme of the gospel and it is therefore the task of an inner city church to be a healing community. The typical urban priority area will by definition have a higher than average proportion of single-parent families, children in care, depressed and disturbed people, people frustrated by unemployment or sick as a result of some aspect of poverty. Such a parish might be called St Luke's, Stressborough. Stressborough is a designated Urban Priority Area. Its nearby industries are run down, resulting in high unemployment. Its overcrowded housing is notorious, and was the subject of a recent TV documentary. Stressborough has a history of racial tension, and it is frequently in the news as a result of the militant stance of its rate-capped Labour Council. The congregation of St Luke's, Stressborough has, not surprisingly, a high number of people within it who are scarred by their environment and in need of healing.

Some members of the congregation of St Luke's Stressborough

Joy

Joy has never been married. She has three children, aged four, three and one, each by a different father. Joy can't cope.

She lives on the edge of breakdown. Until her mother died (aged forty-six) two years ago she had been able to manage, as her mother was a great support. Joy has been severely depressed. She has battered the children on several occasions and has had to keep them away from playgroup in case the bruises were noticed. She hates her flat, on the eighth floor of a tower block. She has difficulty in making her money last from week to week and resorts to giving 'massage' sessions, advertising with a card in the local newsagent's window. She began going to St Luke's after her mother's funeral, though she is by no means regular. Joy is on a high dosage of a major tranquillizer. Her constant anxiety is that her children will be taken into care. She feels 'they are all I have' and is in despair at the idea of losing them.

Stephen

Stephen has been churchwarden for three years. His great desire is to stay churchwarden for another three years, although this means bending a PCC agreement. It is said he has a chip on his shoulder and certainly he is envious of a brother whose success in business he finds hard to take. People feel that Stephen is always trying to prove something. Although he often wears an ingratiating smile and strongly emphasizes the importance of 'welcoming outsiders', people find this patronizing. They are suspicious of his smile because it so easily becomes a snarl, for example when someone sits in his churchwarden's seat. Stephen seems to see other members of the congregation as rivals for his responsibilities rather than as people in their own right. He is easily piqued and has twice resigned his office, while leaving room to be invited back. Deep inside him there seems to be a smouldering anger, although if challenged about this he vehemently denies it. Whatever the explanation, Stephen only seems buoyant when being churchwarden gives him a sense of importance. For this he has plenty of energy. But there are times when others see his face express an unspeakable weight of pain.

Clauda

Clauda is a nurse in the local geriatric hospital. She enjoys her work but she still finds herself resorting to alcohol abuse and periodic bouts of bulimic bingeing on junk food to escape the pain of her life. The drinking came first, when she was a student nurse. But in the last year her bulimia has got worse. Clauda's mother is a black woman but her father was a white policeman. He was a heavy drinker and as a child Clauda witnessed scenes of domestic brutality, not least tirades of racial abuse from her father. Sometimes this was directed to her as much as to her mother. Being married to a black woman did not seem to affect her father's venomous racism. Clauda's mother used to excuse her father saying that he had to 'put up with terrible things at work'. Clauda is bruised and she knows it. At St Luke's she is in charge of the Sunday crèche.

Trev

Trev has always felt more at home with animals than people. He never knew the father his mother refused to talk about. She had a fiery temper and seemed to know no midpoint between indulging him and punishing him. He has always been shy. Now, aged thirty-four, his already low self-esteem can fall no further. For ten years he was employed 'in the Print' as a typesetter. But his firm recently went over to new technology and moved to Swindon. Unemployment in Stressborough runs at 34% for males wanting full-time work. Trev has applied for seventeen jobs since being made redundant but has had no luck, so he can no longer afford to keep his four dogs, to whom he was extremely attached. He became involved with St Luke's after he picked up some part-time work cleaning the church hall windows. Trev is married and has three children. His wife, Stella, is, by contrast, loquacious and, so people say, pushy. She has little time for 'layabouts'. A Girl Guide herself, she runs a small Brownie pack at St Luke's. She doesn't like St Luke's and has as little as possible to do with it. At Christmas she does go to church, but at the Salvation Army.

Lillian

Lillian is eighty-two. She has been a member of St Luke's from childhood. Her arthritis keeps her permanently in a wheelchair so that she can only come to church when the Social Services minibus with a lift is able to bring her, about six times a year. Whenever the vicar visits she is angry he doesn't come more often. Whenever others visit she is angry they are not the vicar. She feels lonely and isolated. There are days when she sees nobody, and doesn't get out of bed. She is afraid of death. But she feels so useless that often she says: 'Death's all I'm good for. Then I'll be no more trouble.' She also says, 'I've tried to pray but it doesn't make any difference. I think God wants us to talk to people not a silver Jesus on a cross on the wall. Still', she goes on, 'there's millions like me aren't there?'

Henry

Henry has recently 'lost his faith'. A few years ago he became very involved at St Luke's. He wanted to be ordained but his preliminary enquiries discouraged him (he is almost illiterate) and he gave up the idea. He works as a hairdresser except when trapped in depressions which sometimes last for weeks. He is gay and feels guilty about this. He is afraid God will punish him for his homosexual relationships. He has been having sessions with a counsellor. He finds them valuable and thinks highly of the counsellor but so far the feelings of guilt remain. Until recently St Luke's was the high spot in his life. His homosexuality is accepted there and he has often been deeply moved by the services, feeling temporary relief from his guilt. He has plenty to do at St Luke's as he finds himself in charge of a weekly Jumble Sale which (except during depressions) he organizes with great fervour. Some people regard this driving, activist side of Henry as compulsive since he doesn't seem to know where to stop and the church hall often looks like a warehouse in a sales boom. Henry does not know why his once lively feelings about 'church' have gone dead inside him. He does not know why the services bore him and somehow irritate him. Meanwhile the guilt and self-hate remain.

Charlie

Charlie was abandoned by his mother soon after his birth. He was brought up in a variety of homes. As a child he showed signs of disturbed behaviour, including violence. He has been regularly admitted to psychiatric hospital. After a spell in prison for breaking the windows of a local health centre he was housed by the Council near St Luke's Church. Charlie has periods when he never speaks. But if someone pays him sincere attention he talks without stopping. Charlie claims his problem is that 'nobody wants to know.' He says, 'I live in a hole where no one goes in and out except me,' and 'I feel like a football, kicked round the field.' And he repeats, frequently, 'They don't understand.' Charlie has made four attempts at suicide.

Ruth

Ruth is a black woman with four children aged ten, eight, seven and three. Her husband died of a heart attack six months ago at the age of forty-three. Her accommodation is damp and inadequate (two bedrooms). She is dependent on Social Security which means she has £28 a week to live on after paying her rent. Ruth and her husband George were very close. George was a bus driver. He tried to organize his shifts so as to be able to help with the children as much as possible. Being such a close-knit family they had never bothered to get to know many other people during their two years in Stressborough. Ruth's grief is still after six months painful beyond words. She shows courage 'for the children's sake' during the day. But the night she spends weeping, awake with the silent howl of her broken heart.

There are seventy-eight people on the electoral roll of St Luke's all of whom carry their own wounds. But Joy, Stephen, Clauda, Trev, Lillian, Henry, Charlie and Ruth have been among those most in need of healing. The question is how St Luke's can be a healing community for them and in order to explore this, let us return to St Luke's some months on and see how for these eight people their church functions as a healing community.

Joy often goes to St Luke's just to be rid of the children for an hour at the crèche. It is the only time in the week she gets any space for herself. Joy doesn't pay any attention to the words of the service, or the sermon. But she sometimes feels what she calls 'peace of mind' in taking communion. She finds the friendly atmosphere of St Luke's attractive and enjoys the coffee after the service more than the service itself. For her, Christian belief, the *Sun* horoscope (of which she is a fan) and 'trying to lead a good life' are mixed up in a jumble. What she likes about St Luke's is that no one tries to force her to 'believe everything it says in the Bible'. On the contrary she feels accepted there. In fact St Luke's is the one place she makes other people laugh (she has a sharp wit), the one place 'I can really enjoy myself'.

St Luke's is still *Stephen's* world. Both his problems and his purpose are bound up with it. Sometimes he wants to move right away, out of the area, as if St Luke's maintained his difficulties. Mostly he takes it for granted. He understands St Luke's as a way of God's work being done in the world, so takes a serious view of his responsibilities. Whatever lies behind his off-putting manner, he is humble enough to feel his duties at St Luke's are a privilege. He may have the reputation of trying to turn St Luke's into 'The Stephen Show' but he senses that he is sinful and, sometimes, worthless. At St Luke's he has some purpose. And this is his life-line, his most reassuring comfort. In his heart he feels that without St Luke's he would be lost.

The Sunday crèche is *Clauda's* joy. She is put under no pressure to run it in any way but her own. She appreciates the acceptance and support at St Luke's but, like Stephen (and Henry), she looks to her church, albeit gropingly, for a deeper reconciliation and for guidance in faith. It is Stephen to whom she has found herself confiding her problems. She feels he really listens to her. She is sure he has told no one else about the bulimia and his discretion means a lot. Several times recently she has been able to avoid going on a food binge by ringing him up and talking about it with him.

Lillian feels angry with the vicar, for visiting her only once a month but that visit nevertheless sustains her sense of belonging to St Luke's which is the last remaining meaning in her life.

Trev's story is more dramatic. One year on from redundancy his confidence and personality have blossomed as a result of his involvement with St Luke's. First he joined a small group (and is now preparing for confirmation), then he was elected a 'sidesperson'. Meanwhile during the day he undertook increasing responsibilities alongside the clergy who were imaginative about tasks, always encouraging, and who enjoyed his company, not seeming to notice his shyness. This easy contact with other people is new to Trev. He knew it neither in his family nor at work. He feels happier now, though being out of work is a running sore. Above all he has surprised himself (not to mention Stella) by his increased ability to be sociable and involved. He has started going to the pub by himself which Stella says is even more 'not like you, Trev' than his going to church.

The vicar, Gerald Perkins, is not surprised that *Henry* has lost his faith. He was almost expecting it, and is not discouraged, whilst recognizing how painful it is for Henry. Henry's faith had been in a vengeful, punishing God who bore little resemblance to the God of the New Testament. Gerald's hope is that Henry's loss of faith might herald new faith in a more accepting, forgiving God. For it is healing from guilt that Henry seems to need. This is where St Luke's is helping him most. It is because the services include a theme of forgiveness that they have meant so much to him. Henry's feelings of guilt run very deep. He may need a long period of counselling as well as the consistent support of his church to enable the inner reconciliation he needs. Counselling by itself might not be enough. Henry's religious nature looks for a community of faith. His humanity looks for an extended family (which he otherwise does not have) where he can fit in and express different sides of himself. In providing this St Luke's is important to him.

Charlie became involved at St Luke's after meeting Henry at the Launderette. Henry found him difficult to shake off. He only succeeded in doing so by leaving him, an hour later, at the St Luke's mid-morning Eucharist. Charlie interrupted the service several times until the vicar told him very firmly that if he didn't stop shouting he would have to leave. He also told

him that the service would be finished in ten minutes and
added that if Charlie were quiet he could then have coffee
with everyone else and there would be a chance to talk.

It seems that what attracts Charlie to St Luke's is being
accepted. His odd behaviour, such as occasionally shouting
out or peering very closely at objects for a long time doesn't
stop members of the congregation from talking to him. When
he starts to drivel he is sometimes told to 'shut up Charlie',
and there are frequently affectionate jokes at his expense. But
he is not left out of parish events. And he is encouraged to
make his own contribution. (This became easier after it was
discovered he could sing quite well.) St Luke's finds him hard
to manage. He can be frustrating, stubborn and demanding.
Belonging to St Luke's has not led to any dramatic instances
of healing for Charlie. But, so far anyhow, he has had to
return to hospital less often. It is hard to know for certain
what St Luke's means to Charlie. He seems to take it for
granted now as part of his life.

Ruth sometimes feels isolated at St Luke's. She often has
the sense that nobody notices her pain. People say, 'How
brave you are', or, 'Aren't your children marvellous!' but
rarely come close to her grief. On the other hand Enid, the
woman deacon, is her greatest support. Ruth joked to her one
Sunday, 'The children lost George but thanks to you they
haven't lost me as well'.

In its ministry in Stressborough St Luke's both fails and
succeeds as a healing community. It fails, for example, when
Ruth is left feeling that no one has noticed her pain. It fails to
free Charlie of his mental handicap. So far it has failed to
help Henry feel reconciled to his God or himself. It has failed
to heal Trev's wound of unemployment, and failed to prevent
Lillian's loneliness. It has not cured Clauda's alcoholism,
Stephen's lack of self-esteem or Joy's depression. It is
successful as a healing community, however, on two levels.
There is healing benefit in belonging to St Luke's as a
community of fellow human beings. On another level there
are healing benefits in belonging to a Christian fellowship
with its distinctive faith and hope. Theologically these two
levels are inseparable but for purposes of description it is
useful to distinguish between them. For healing does not

always depend on faith. It is assisted by antibiotics and by humour. On the level of human fellowship St Luke's contributes to its members' healing by being accepting, supportive and friendly, a place to belong. This is an important aspect of healing. Christians are mistaken when they imagine that Christ's healing Spirit must always advertise its work like a neon sign on a factory. Healing in a congregation is usually unobtrusive, gradual, almost imperceptible, like the slow rise of Trev's self-esteem over more than a year. St Luke's is a healing community by being a place of listening, laughter and common human warmth.

It is also a healing community as a result of its Christian faith and hope. A sociologist would categorize Joy's faith as belonging more to 'common' than 'conventional' religion. Certainly her faith is confused, inarticulate, and dim. But the 'peace of mind' she has felt at communion is a balm she associates with church and with 'religion'. For her it has something to do with God. And who is to say it has not? Stephen's faith is more explicit. The consolation he finds through St Luke's derives primarily from his faith and the sustenance of this by the services of the Church. For Trev the two levels of human fellowship and Christian belief are an inseparable mixture. His confidence has been built up by means of the humanity he has experienced at St Luke's. But his new interest in Christian faith is important to him. He believes he has a journey of discovery to make and because of St Luke's he will be able to make it. These examples illustrate how it is sometimes by virtue of its distinctive Christian faith that St Luke's functions as a healing community. And of course the examples could be greatly multiplied. Gerald Perkins, middle-of-the-road Anglican vicar, does not object to occasional services of healing on which a prominent lay woman in the congregation (a member of the Bishop's Committee for Healing) is so keen. Other members of the church visit the elderly, which they see as connected with the church's ministry of healing, and someone on the PCC who happens to be a social worker is trying to start a Christian support group for depressed single mothers. But if St Luke's is to grow as a healing community and move beyond the present attempts of some of its members to assist healing in isolated instances, the congregation as a whole needs to gain a much deeper theological understanding of what it means to be 'in Christ'.

Life 'in Christ'

St Luke's has yet to discover as a congregation the vision of health offered in the Old and New Testaments, that vision which is distinctively revealed in the Bible, which can become a driving vision for those who learn to be inspired by it. The central characteristic of this view of health is that it is corporate.[2] The health of one person affects the health of others and cannot be considered apart from others. Health is corporate because salvation is corporate and health and salvation belong together. Lying behind this is the assumption that God has created a world in which human beings must share their resources, including their health, to find fulfilment. So, in the Old Testament we find that gifts or vocations are not given to individuals for the sake of that individual alone but for the community. Moses, for example, was not called back into Egypt for the sake of his own soul but to do a job for the Hebrews with whom he was identified. God's promise in the Old Testament is to the whole people, as the declaration to Abraham shows: 'I will establish my covenant between me and thee, and thy seed after thee, throughout generations for an everlasting covenant' (Gen. 17.7). And once he has called his people, we hear in the rest of the Old Testament how God leads, sustains, loves, punishes and saves them. The whole story illustrates a corporate vocation. The great saving acts which formed the people of Israel, the Passover, the Exodus, the giving of the Law on Sinai and winning the Promised Land are all corporate, communal events.

The New Testament takes up the theme: 'As in Adam *all* die, so in Christ shall *all* be made alive' (1 Cor. 15.22) (my italics). Interrelation in community is evoked by the imagery of the vine with its many branches from one stem (John 15.5f.) or 'the body', with its interdependent members. In order to understand Christ's healing miracles fully, moreover, it is important to see Christ as healer, the sick person and the witnesses as all representing the community. It is because of the underlying corporate reference that Christ's public signs proclaim 'good news' beyond their immediate situation and are able to carry a clear message for the whole of humanity. Just as Jeremiah had smashed the earthenware jar before the elders in the Valley of Benhinnom (Jer. 19.1 – 12) as a public sign of what God, in his anger, intended to do to the people, so Jesus too performed a series of acts whose public nature had meaning for the whole community who were witness to them.[3] Just as Hosea had married a whore as a concrete and public expression of Israel's infidelity to Yahweh (Hos. 1.2) or the Evangelists portray John the Baptist as dressed in the same manner as Elijah to demonstrate his status as a prophet before all the people (2 Kings 1.8, cf. Mark 1.6), so Jesus performs the symbolic acts of a prophet at the Last Supper bequeathing to the Church the signs which it has enacted ever since as the Eucharist.

The Evangelists use Christ's miracles to show him demonstrating in public God's immediate intentions and starting to put them into practice. Inevitably they demand a response from the people they address. They are a *crisis* for those who witness them. They offer salvation to those who see the coming Kingdom for what it is, repent, and find their life renewed. Others make the wrong choice and are lost (Matt. 11.20, Luke 10.3, 17.12, John 9.39, 11). The early Church soon discovered that identification with the sick (Acts 3.18 – 23) means the Church suffering also (Acts 4.3). The New Testament proclaims a Christ who is able to bear my suffering. But in so far as *I* am joined to Christ I open myself to participate in the suffering of others. Christ's announcement of salvation from sin/sickness/death/judgement, leads to new life in Christ as a remade person living in a new kind of Kingdom. This 'new life' is a commitment of the whole person to be in Christ and to let Christ be in you as a man and woman commit themselves in marriage to be one flesh, for better, for worse, in sickness and in health. It is to assent to what Christ has done in joining himself to all sick, sinful people.

To the extent that St Luke's congregation can discover afresh the radical solidarity of this view of shared health their self-understanding as a healing community will be effectively enhanced. One of the most crippling diseases in the inner city is the prevalence of a style of life in which people are socialized to understand their self-identity without reference to other people. Christian faith, by contrast, should lead to a perception of one's self in the light of an awareness of the experience of others. (If society at large embraced this view it would not permit the inner city environment to continue.) Christians have a responsibility to challenge the individualism of the age by remembering the corporate nature of human interdependence as equally beloved children of the same heavenly Father. What this means for St Luke's is that the others learn to live alongside Charlie or Clauda or Henry recognizing their own sin and suffering as joined to theirs. It means Lillian's loneliness or Ruth's grief is not just 'their problem' but a limit on the health of them all.

In this New Testament view of health men and women are raised to hope by the belief that God brings good out of evil and healing out of suffering. This is an insight which can transform *any* medical situation from bitterness to joy. But it is not automatic. It presupposes Christian faith. For example, after an accident a person may regain full health but remain bitter, cursing God and society, and bringing sorrow to family and friends. Another person may remain crippled but become kinder, developing a power of empathy. Christians see suffering in the light of atonement. That is, as bound up with Christ's obedient response to suffering 'even unto death'. God did not take the cross away. He continues to use it to work for the salvation of humankind. The suffering of Christ, it is believed, was not in vain. With such a faith sickness may always be seen as an opportunity to join in partnership with God in his great plan: to use sickness for the salvation of all by throwing your life, including your suffering, in with God, who is able to overcome even the last enemy, death. This is a radical and challenging faith. But these are the terms in which St Paul describes his faith (2 Cor. 4.7–5.5.) and it need be no less potent a faith for the congregation of St Luke's. First-century Corinth had no more reason to embrace Paul's vision than Stressborough today. Faith like Paul's has never been fashionable.

Awareness of what prevents or helps healing

In order to grow as a healing community St Luke's needs to

become more pastorally aware of what promotes or prevents healing. Some things in their present congregational life make matters worse rather than better. The people who, either ostentatiously or quietly, avoid Stephen because he's so often 'prickly' do not help him to feel more at home with himself. They rather provoke him to bolster his self-esteem by acting out his show of power more defensively. Nevertheless their present avoidance is understandable. There is a natural fear of conflict. It is the fear of facing the uncomfortable aftermath of a row in which verbal wounds are inflicted but left festering on both sides. Even when feelings of conflict are shared sensitively it is easy to be left feeling incomplete. On the other hand when conflict is not able to be shared it can lead to a thoroughly poisoned relationship. As far as possible, therefore, conflict in a congregation should be expressed rather than excommunicated. When conflict is felt between two people they will find it less difficult to share if they feel it will not lead to general rejection but be contained: held by the understanding and support of the minister or others. However, it is frightening to share anger, hurt feelings or criticism. So while it is important for pastors not to be thrown by conflict, and sometimes to be midwife to it, it is unrealistic to be too disappointed when a particular conflict cannot be faced, such as when members of the congregation resent Stephen's bossiness but are unable to tell him.

Something else at St Luke's which hinders rather than helps is Trev's wife Stella's uncontrollable anger. When she is met by a problem, such as the hall being left untidy on Brownies' night, Stella finds herself caught in an automatic response of fury. Her angry feelings pour out like molten ore. Next day or a week later the mention of the incident is sufficient to set her off again. What response will be better rather than worse for Stella? It will help her if the pastor is able to show some sympathy for the cause of Stella's anger whilst nevertheless remaining rational and proportional to the problem in his or her own response. It will help if the pastor is not 'thrown' by Stella's anger, and therefore does not signal to her any judgement on the irrationality of her response which she may already recognize and despise but not be able to control.

Finally, the 'not noticing' of pain which Ruth felt so keenly

is the cause of much missed opportunity for healing at St
Luke's. It would be helpful, for instance, if someone noticed
the story behind Stephen's behaviour and asked what inner
conflict it might represent. What does it mean, for example,
that he welcomes 'outsiders' so patronizingly? Learning to
hear the 'music behind the words' is a pastoral prerequisite
for healing and for any kind of care. We shall explore this in
more detail in Chapter Eleven which describes a programme
of pastoral training for the whole congregation.

Conclusion

An inner city church can be a healing community, but within
limits. If my humanity is fundamentally damaged because,
like Charlie, I have never known a satisfying relationship in
my life then the healing I need, however loving my new
environment, is likely to take many years. In practice this
means that an inner city congregation representative of its
parish is bound to contain within its membership a mixture
of personalities who are disturbed, aggressive, depressive
and self-obsessed. No congregation will be an ideal healing
community. But it is important for an inner city congregation
to recognize the particular burden of suffering it is likely to
find itself carrying.

Healing in the congregation can be significant but only
partial where wounds are maintained by the inner city
environment. This implies that a congregation attends to the
healing of 'structures' as well as individual people. When
Jesus healed the leper he not only cured the person but
challenged the political and religious establishment which
had put that person beyond salvation. The task of healing in
the inner city will involve the development of a prophetic and
political stance in response to the social structures which
cause or maintain poor health. Chapter Ten discusses the
question of the political involvement of a UPA congregation.

The purpose of being a healing community is not to
establish a cosy 'healed' fellowship of the 'saved' but to
collaborate with God's healing spirit in the wider purpose of
building God's Kingdom. This means remaining wounded as
inner city people are wounded. It means discovering the
nature of God's solidarity with his human creatures, whilst at

the same time glimpsing and participating in the wholeness of the heavenly city—eternal life with Christ in God: 'When anyone is united to Christ, there is a new world; the old order has gone, and a new order has already begun' (2 Cor. 5.17).

Notes

1. D. Bonhoeffer, *Life Together,* SCM 1983, p. 18.
2. For a comprehensive discussion of this issue see R. A. Lambourne, *Community, Church and Healing,* Darton, Longman and Todd 1963, to which this chapter is indebted.
3. See, for example, John 5.1 — 17.

SEVEN

A Serving Community

'Our collective view is that a different approach is needed.
We believe that Churches in the UPAs have to become
local, *outward-looking* and *participating* churches.'

Faith in the City[1]

Discovering the task of service

The Good Samaritan. Jesus washing his disciples' feet. 'Love
your neighbour as yourself.' The New Testament ideal of
service is something individual Christians are brought up to
interpret on a daily basis. Life constantly provides opportunities for individual acts of care within the family, at school
or work, in the neighbourhood, or by charitable giving to
faraway places. On this view, responsibility for acts of service
lies with the individual. Much Christian service takes place in
this way. In our individualistic society it is its most obvious
interpretation. The human needs in a UPA parish are met
more effectively, however, if the Church as a body organizes
a considered response. Its congregation needs to explore how,
by working together, they can become a serving community.
In order to do this, they will need to decide what responses
are in fact appropriate for a church to make to needs in the
parish, a hotly debated and debatable subject, which
nevertheless they cannot afford to ignore. The purpose of this
chapter is to discuss some key issues central to this debate
and so central to any UPA church's consideration of how best
to serve its parish. These issues cover a broad scope and
there will inevitably be a spread of interest in this chapter as
we move from topic to topic. The chapter first considers the
symbolic role of the Church in the minds of parishioners.
Then it summarizes *Faith in the City*'s recommendations on
how a UPA church can serve its parish before moving to a

discussion of use of buildings and the requirements of a strategy for parish pastoral care. The chapter concludes with an illustration of how one member of a church which had succeeded in planning such a strategy learned to serve her parish by taking part in the task of preparing parishioners for baptism.

Serving the expectations of parishioners

In his book *The Priestlike Task* Wesley Carr writes: 'A church is consciously prepared to be used symbolically, and at times uncomfortably, on behalf of the society of which it is a part.'[2] He argues that in order to discover its service task a church should evaluate its internal life in relation to the parish setting and should consider the way these two interact. He suggests that they will find that parishioners focus their hopes and fears on the Church, often unconsciously, and argues that a church must become aware of these in order to discover its task. Such hopes may be irrational, he writes, 'manifested at points where life and human experience seem potentially beyond control', such as death, the ultimate boundary of life which parishioners hope will be managed by the church. Carr goes on:

> The level of people's participation in public religion bears little correlation to the degree of their expectation that the church stands competently at points of serious transition and adjustment in the course of life and finally of death.[3]

And he considers that the basis of the church's ministry is to handle competently such dependent expectations of parishioners.[4]

Research into attitudes in Tower Hamlets presents a challenge to this interpretation. Few of those interviewed put any hope in the church: 'Too much bleeding church don't do you any good,' said a retired baker who had been brought up in a Church of England children's home.[5] About three-quarters of the sample had never seen their local Church of England vicar, and over a half had never been aware of a Church of England vicar of any kind.[6] These facts contrast with the 'powerfulness of the expectations which may be focused in the minister' which Wesley Carr assumes.

Nevertheless, even in Tower Hamlets there is evidence that rites of passage retain at least vestigial significance. Unlike the Church of England as an institution, rites of passage are still 'us' as well as 'them'. And Carr is clearly right in pointing to the emotional and usually unconscious expectations of inner city people who approach the church in connection with a baptism, marriage or a funeral. He is right, too, to emphasize the importance of appreciating what this means for the church's task of service.

To achieve this appreciation there has to be clear thinking about the relationship of pastoral care, evangelism and a church's understanding of rites of passage. Sociological research points to 'an increasing number of people susceptible to the ideas of common religion without the direction that comes from more or less regular contact with at least some orthodox teaching'.[7] This suggests as an aim for the Church 'to create contexts in which "belief" can emerge from a semi-conscious level and be gradually transformed into something closer to an authentic Christian faith'.[8] It is an aim endorsed by *Faith in the City*.[9] But is this evangelical aim compatible with appropriate pastoral care? What if a family passionately want their baby baptized but do not have the least interest in Christian orthodoxy? There is a tension between mission and ministry. *Mission* is concerned to proclaim, to call for repentance and change on account of the gospel. *Ministry's* text is St Mark's depiction of Jesus as coming 'not to be served but to serve and to give his life as a ransom for many' (Mark 10.45). It is this side of the tension that is illustrated in Wesley Carr's expectations of a church. To the extent that a desire for baptism and other rites of passage is culturally embedded in our society, the Church of the land will naturally want to associate itself as far as possible with that desire. Commenting on the following interview with a roadsweeper in Tower Hamlets, Geoffrey Ahern writes: 'The church shoots itself in the foot with its sectarian retreat into a strict baptism policy. How can theologians answer the roadsweeper satisfactorily?'[10]

I said to the preacher when I had my baby baptised (he found another clergyman to do it), 'I don't go to church.' He said, 'Well, I'm not baptising.' I said, 'Why not?' He said,

'You don't go to church.' . . . 'What's that to do with that?' I said, 'I'm asking you to baptise my child,' I said, '*I* don't believe in it, there's nothing to say my child don't believe in it'. . . To me, baptism is a key to the door, to church . . . Every man and every woman has got a mind of its own . . . but that mind's got to come from the beginning. You've got to put that little seed there . . .[11]

For Wesley Carr 'Service as self-giving indicates the way in which the surrender of control is of the essence of ministry.'[12] He suggests a consultancy model of ministry as a way of using rites of passage to serve parishioners' needs, and this is indeed a promising model. Those involved with parishioners in rites of passage, on this model, aim to enable them to understand the meaning of the rite but leave them free to respond on their own authority. This approach does justice both to the Church's ambition to proclaim the God celebrated in rites of passage and to the autonomy of the parishioner whose approach to the rite may be muddled or semi-pagan. However, in so far as the Church representative (whether clerical or lay) speaks a truth which is in harmony with the parishioner's own experience then *Faith in the City*'s aim for the Church to nurture 'common belief in God towards an authentic Christian faith'[13] is promoted.

This resolution of the discontinuity between mission and ministry is vital, since one of the most obvious ways for an inner city church to serve its parish is by responding sensitively to requests for baptisms, marriages and funerals. However, in a UPA parish of, say, 20,000 people this implies a prodigious quantity of pastoral work requiring the efforts of as many of the congregation as possible, which is why Chapter Twelve of this book is given over to describing a pastoral visiting scheme for the whole congregation.

'Faith in the City' and the task of service

Faith in the City emphasizes the importance of *neighbourhood* as a primary unit for the Church's ministry and mission.[14] It suggests the need to revise parochial boundaries to relate more closely to those parts of a locality understood by residents as 'neighbourhoods'. This recommendation under-lines the importance of a parochial system to ensure the Church's presence in the inner city. The disadvantage of the arbitrariness by which people on one side of a street at a parish's edge must marry in St Botolph's while their neighbours opposite belong to St Chad's is offset by the pastoral advantages of working a specific patch which enables the Church to organize pastoral care within set boundaries. Some members of the congregation may commute from another parish, but this does not affect the responsibility of that congregation to concentrate its pastoral care on its own parish. Commuters share this responsibility. As the result of its contacts through rites of passage, hospitals, schools, pubs, institutions and agencies, the local newspaper and word of mouth, the potential call for pastoral care from an inner city congregation is limitless. It is not just people in crisis or those 'at points of serious transition and adjustment' who need the Church's care but the chronically sick, lonely, depressed, anxious, frustrated and angry.

However a local church chooses to interact with and serve its parish, it starts with a considerable asset in its premises. The possession of *plant* equips every church with a specific means of serving the parish. Parishioners are able to come on their own initiative to use whatever the church provides. This may be a simple service such as giving help in writing a letter or filling in a form. It might be giving food to homeless callers, providing a warm room where tea is available, or holding a jumble sale. It is normal to think of church plant as a drain on resources, but in a UPA all premises are themselves a crucial resource. The question of how plant is used, of course, must be a matter for ecumenical and inter-agency collaboration. The necessity and virtue of co-operation in projects involving employment, housing, social care and community work is obvious. The very process of identifying the needs of a parish presupposes collaboration. So does any project trying to make best use of resources. When churches, tenants' associations, community agencies and local people of no particular affiliation plan together imaginative and realistic projects are born. I have known children's holiday schemes, a drop-in centre, bereavement projects and youth work take shape in this way. Current social concerns such as the care of psychiatric patients released into the 'community', increased homelessness, unemployment and racism can only be effectively responded to by an alliance of the professional, voluntary and residential community who make up the whole (see Chapter Eleven, 'On Political Involvement'). By contrast the negative consequences and missed opportunities of isolation can be grave, as for example, when a church launches an expensive appeal for its roof without considering the option of collaborating with a neighbouring denomination whose church is new and frequently vacant.

The church in the inner city has a long history of involvement with parish pastoral care schemes. Church schools and the provision of housing have accompanied parish work since the onset of industrial urban development. Moral welfare projects such as the Josephine Butler scheme or University and Public School Settlements provide additional examples. But different styles of projects have been fashionable at different times during this history and criticism is easy with hindsight. Aims and resources have of course varied and still do. Most recently *Faith in the City* presented its views on UPA parish church projects but since these are spread across three hundred pages of that book I have attempted to summarize them in highly compressed form below.

Work[15]

Fearing persistent high unemployment in UPAs *Faith in the City* sees the challenge to churches as helping to promote work (defined in short as 'doing something useful' for yourself or others) which the community will value and which confers a degree of self-respect, such as work in and around the home. The church should support initiatives such as Church Action with the Unemployed to bring about the necessary 'self-provisioning' of tools and training. It can offer its resources of people, premises and equipment in such schemes.

Housing[16]

Local church participation in housing schemes involves

collaboration with housing associations, many of which originated from the initiative of local councils of churches. *Faith in the City* mentions, for example, 'the London Churches Resettlement Agency, launched in 1984 jointly by the Bishop of London and Cardinal Hume, to help release the human resources of local congregations who want to provide small-scale housing at a local level for homeless people.'

Social Care[17]

Here *Faith in the City* asks local UPA churches to become deeply aware of the poverty and social need within the parish and to be clear about the values and nature of public policy's response. They must resist the temptation to pursue church life without any serious relationship to the neighbourhood, and the temptation to see members more in terms of what they do for the church than for the parish. Learning to understand the work of local professional workers is important. For example they may be invited to talk to the congregation. Church members can be trained to provide a local service for bereaved, handicapped, elderly or house-bound people, or to respond to problems in housing, local transport, schooling or policing. *Faith in the City* mentions with approval the 255 voluntary Victim Support Schemes operating in Britain which all depend on local initiatives in multi-agency collaboration.

Community Work[18]

Community work is not about providing services to people. It 'seeks to involve those concerned in purposeful action to change their situation; community work intervention is *with* rather than *for* people.' *Faith in the City* sees a local church's contribution to community work as the activity of lay people in tenants' associations, community councils, action groups or groups of the elderly or the young. They will need encouragement to manage the 'strange alliances, hard decisions and necessary compromises' this will involve. Support from the diocese is crucial though it must not impose solutions.

Education[19]

The headmaster of a comprehensive school in a tough area of the West Midlands wrote to the *Faith in the City* commission: 'I am now aware that quiet friendship, prayer and patient support by the Church of those in the "firing line" day by day can be valuable out of all proportion to its appearance.' A group of East London primary school teachers similarly submitted their doubt 'whether they would have survived the stress and strain of their work had it not been for the support of local Anglican clergy and lay people.'

Faith in the City comments on the 'degree of goodwill towards the Church' which results from the sensitive support of local schools by the parish church. Teachers, for example, appreciate the assistance of local clergy in contacting the leaders of other faiths. Church members can participate in language projects. All churches can be open to learning about the other faiths and cultures in their community.

Young People[20]

The prime responsibility for work with young people in the Church of England is at parish level. It is ultimately the parishes who decide what kind of provision is to be offered, and appoint either voluntary or paid staff to work with young people. Many local churches can be focal points in neighbourhoods, and this can enable immediate responses to be made to local schools.

Faith in the City strongly advocates working with young people *outside* the church. It refers to the

sizeable groups of young people who are trapped in UPAs, who only gain attention when they become a threat, who are denied equality of opportunity and life chances, and with whom the Churches have little or no contact.

The report continues:

It is difficult to exaggerate how alienated these young people are: from adult ideas of how young people should behave; from their peers of different social classes; from agencies they think of acting on adults' behalf and not usually in the interests of young people e.g. from the police; from school and from the Church.

The effective work of open youth clubs has often turned more to providing 'club nights' for its own members: 'The task of sustaining open youth clubs has proved just too tough.' Parishes now require support and training, e.g. by the Frontier Youth Trust. But *Faith in the City* recommends that the Board of Education and the Diocesan Youth Officers work towards a national strategy for this work.

Mobilizing for the task of service

Faith in the City suggests that UPA congregations corporately plan a strategy to develop the life of the church, 'maybe using particular groups, but always involving the whole congregation in the final decisions,'[21] (see Chapter Eight below). 'Changes', it says, 'should be accomplished gradually over a period of years with careful monitoring and discussions.' Planning a strategy presupposes knowledge of local needs as they are and hence of vigorous analysis. *Faith in the City* provides an 'audit for the local church'[22] to help it 'understand itself in its situation, reflect on its purpose, and then make plans for becoming a more effective, outward-looking and participating church'. The audit suggests making a large map of the parish showing details of housing, transport and meeting places. It suggests the map be accompanied by a statistical profile (using census data and with the help of local authorities) of the parishioners according to age, sex, employment, ethnic groups and mobility, together with information about what people feel about the area, what conflicts there are and who makes the decisions which affect it. A questionnaire is provided to help build an accurate picture of the local church.

The purpose of *Faith in the City's* audit is to provide a corporate analysis by the congregation as a basis for common planning. But individual members of the congregation also need to consider what belonging to the church means to them. There is the important question of how the church serves 'me' as a person and how my needs are met by belonging, as well as that of how I can serve others. This is likely to prompt further questions about connections: do my beliefs, worship and fellowship express themselves in appropriate service, for example? Or do I feel I have the balance right in my responsibilities to myself, my family, work, church and other commitments? For some people it is a major shift to move from the idea of 'going to church' to that of belonging, however loosely, to a team of people with certain responsibilities for pastoral care in the parish. They will need help to understand how such an idea connects with their experience and present assumptions. Some people, for example, may already visit the elderly on their block regularly and feel this to be as much visiting as they can manage. They would rightly be hostile to the idea of the church apparently making a demand for *more* visiting in the name of its own schemes. Both needs and resources must therefore be analysed, including awareness of what the present caring involvement of the church comprises and what is unrealized potential.

A parish strategy for corporate pastoral care requires firm theological and psychological foundations. A church whose religious growth has become blocked can nevertheless express itself in a programme of energetic activism. Dutiful or patronizing caring, or care to placate guilty feelings will lead only to distress. The distinctive quality of Christian pastoral care is its rootedness in God: 'We love because he first loved us' (1 John 4.19). But this very fact causes a tension. Some wish to place emphasis on the church as a *presence* in the parish, concentrating on worship and assisting parishioners to understand and manage their ultimate dependence on God. This primary task can easily be displaced, it is said, and the true identity of the Church lost, by a too obvious alignment with social causes. For others an active involvement in care schemes and social projects follows obviously from commitment to the two great commandments.

This theological tension is something a congregation needs to think about and analyse in the light of their own history and circumstances. Without due self-understanding churches are blown about in the prevailing winds of ideological fashion. The pastoral care of the sixties, for example, is now criticized for a too easy identification with the current vogue of ego-fulfilment for the individual, an ideal of secular humanism that is too narrow for Christianity. Loss of theological confidence in that decade led to the cutting of ties with the long, but temporarily ignored, classical tradition of pastoral care.[23] Similarly in UPA churches of a liberal kind, the influence of John Robinson's *Honest to God,*[24] Harvey Cox's *The Secular City*[25] and other exploratory writings, while sowing the seeds of a creative renewal still felt today, encouraged a tendency to place heaven above the community centre. Spirituality became seen as the power of the newly-founded neighbourhood newspaper to 'affirm the area' and tenants' association meetings were preferred to church fellowship. The pastoral task was seen as supporting the work of secular and community social activities rather than initiating church-based pastoral care. The desire was to ring down the curtain on an era which had rightly come to be perceived as both imperialistic and paternalistic on the part of the Church.

This fashion of the Sixties illustrates how strongly underlying assumptions can influence church planning. It also happens to be the climate of my own first years in UPA ministry and one I have reacted against. My experience suggests that a congregation serves its parish by being itself, a church congregation, to the best of its ability. It is the Church's vision of God and the potential for pastoral care released by the gospel which is a congregation's distinctive contribution to their parish. Human warmth of any kind expresses this. It is important not to retreat from 'incarnation' to mere 'proclamation'. Nevertheless the *whole* life of the church, including its worship, prayer, openness to learning, and struggle to live 'in Christ' is the church's resource in serving its parish, not just the explicit outworking of this in a pastoral strategy. So it is a valid instinct which senses that the elusive whole life of the church matters most, however diffuse its expression. But it does not follow that there is therefore no need to plan policies and order priorities. Without them outdated habits and attachments cannot be sloughed off and rethought.

The power of tradition is formidable. Well-established routines maintain themselves. If the choir has visited the same campsite for years, a project which has absorbed the lion's share of church energy during August, it may be hard for that parish to transfer their support to understaffed playschemes on local estates, even though the choir camp is now for a quarter of its original number and mostly for children from outside the parish. The needs of an inner city parish are so broad in range, and so profound, that without determining priorities the church's energy is likely to be consumed in a continuously changing pattern of instant responses to immediate crises which sap morale and lead in various ways to exhaustion. An equally unfortunate consequence of failing to plan is that the parish may be held at the mercy of one or two people, a bullying vicar perhaps, or an obsessive member of the PCC. The corporate planning described in the next chapter reduces the risk of both exhaustion and domination and is also a key aspect of the congregation's development as a fellowship 'in Christ'. The discussion, disagreements and open conflict involved, though painful, enable those who take part to make much more of a personal investment in the life of the church than if they were passive members. It is a means of learning and growth.

In this way, individual members of the congregation/community come to make real to themselves the task of service. For many, like Norah, a parishioner at St Atusquo's, the experience proves a watershed. Norah reluctantly agreed to take part in a parish analysis, but doubted the value of the exercise. She thought St Atusquo's had always managed quite well without this 'analysis' the new vicar was so keen on. Nevertheless she found herself facing a series of questions in discussion with others which, she had to admit, had opened her eyes. She had never known there was a home for the mentally handicapped in the next street from her own. She didn't realize the church opposite the park housed a Baptist congregation. She thought it had closed down. And she had no idea how high unemployment was among young, especially black, people in the parish. More personally Norah discovered that in twelve years at St Atusquo she had never once shared what her faith meant to her (and it meant a lot) with anyone else. Nor would she have felt confident enough in herself or her faith to begin to try. This question had arisen in connection with the possibility of a team of people helping in baptism preparation. This was in itself a startling idea to Norah who had never considered that anyone other than the vicar was allowed, never mind able, to be involved in baptism preparation. But this had been her most significant eye-opener; she had hitherto never dreamed that the scope of the vicar's work was so vast (see Chapter Nine). She now saw that he could not possibly respond to the pastoral needs of the parish by himself. She began to wonder if even a small army of volunteers would suffice. As a result of her new perceptions Norah, with great hesitation, joined a small group of church members willing to visit or be visited by a family who wanted their child baptized.

Although Norah had prepared to receive her first family by attending two group sessions arranged by the PCC, she was nevertheless very nervous beforehand. She soon relaxed. The couple who came, bringing the baby, were the baby's mother (a single parent) and *her* mother. The conversation flowed easily. Norah said straightforwardly that she couldn't talk a lot about what she believed. She said that going to church meant a lot to her. She had found support there at the time of her father's cancer. Norah was surprised how comfortable she felt. She was not asked difficult questions to which she didn't know the answer. And she felt rather pleased when, at the end, the baby's mother admitted she hadn't really wanted to come but was now very glad she had. She told Norah she hadn't thought church people were as 'normal' as Norah. And she looked forward to seeing her on Sunday. Norah had discovered that her participation in the work of analysis and planning led to a way of sharing her faith which was both satisfying for her and helpful to others. Norah felt she had become part of a serving community.

Notes

1. *Faith in the City,* p. 74.
2. W. Carr, *The Priestlike Task,* SPCK 1985, p. 26.
3. ibid., p. 10.
4. Following the arguments and research of B. Reed, *The Dynamics of Religion,* Darton Longman and Todd 1978, as acknowledged by Carr, p. 12.

5. G. Ahern and G. Davie, *Inner City of God,* Hodder and Stoughton 1987, p. 34.
6. ibid., p. 102.
7. ibid., p. 59.
8. ibid., p. 61.
9. *Faith in the City,* p. 66.
10. Ahern and Davie, p. 127.
11. ibid., pp. 99—100.
12. Carr, p. 9.
13. *Faith in the City,* p. 66.
14. ibid., p. 93.
15. ibid., pp. 224—226.
16. ibid., pp. 257f.
17. ibid., pp. 278, 279.
18. ibid., pp. 284—289.
19. ibid., pp. 301—307.
20. ibid., pp. 315—322.
21. ibid., p. 376.
22. For references concerning the audit see *Faith in the City* pp. 367—372. This audit is now being revised by the staff of the Archbishop's Officer for Urban Priority Areas (Prebendary Patrick Dearnley), Church House, Great Smith St., London SW1P 3NZ.
23. See T. C. Oden, *Care of Souls in the Classic Tradition,* Philadelphia, Fortress 1984.
24. J. A. T. Robinson, *Honest to God,* SCM 1963.
25. H. Cox, *The Secular City,* Penguin 1968.

PART THREE

The Management and Development of an Inner City Church's Ministry

Introduction

I hope that this book's argument so far has presented a realistic and clear picture of the context and content of a UPA church's task.

An inner city church is set in a brutalized environment and surrounded by a sea of human need. Crushing though this environment can be, it nevertheless fails to extinguish people's warmth, humour and vitality. Indeed the drama of city life is played against a back-drop rich in human diversity and is able to express a certain solidarity of feeling. Side by side with poverty and human deprivation are found generosity and a striking spontaneity and openness of spirit. To the inner city the Church brings the stories, teaching, symbols and ceremonies of its tradition to celebrate God in its midst. The common life described in this tradition is capable of expression in a fellowship which gives an enhanced sense of belonging and self-acceptance, and offers an extended family in which people can make friends and find fulfilment.

The church in the inner city can provide a community of healing and human growth. As its congregation struggles corporately with prayer, the tradition of faith and its own difficulties and human conflict the church continues to learn and be surprised by the 'life in Christ' revealed in the New Testament. The church is able to lead people from alienation to reconciliation and from despair to hope. After analysis and corporate planning, and in collaboration with other agencies, the church is able to respond to the expectations and needs of parishioners with whatever resources it has.

To realize its full potential for ministry will of course require a church to organize and plan appropriate structures. How will decisions to be made to introduce change and who will make them? What is to be the role of those who are ordained ministers? If tasks are to be shared and mutual

117

support is required then small groups will be needed. But might they not stray from the course and prove difficult to lead? And there are further questions: What will happen when the church touches on political issues? Will it not be necessary to offer pastoral training to the congregation? And what might the church become as a result of all this?

EIGHT

Management, Structures and Decision Making

Quod omnes tangit, ab omnibus tractari debet. Things
that affect all must be dealt with by all (legal phrase of
ecclesiastical tradition).[1]

The purpose of this chapter is to examine what is involved in
managing the ministry of an inner city church, what structures
may be needed and how the congregation as a whole can
contribute to decision-making. The debate about this subject
has moved fast and far during the last forty years. In *The
Parish in Action*[2] Joost de Blank described his experiment
with the parish conference in 1948/9. Paul Moore's *The
Church Reclaims the City*[3] (1964) describes his pioneering
work as rector in an American slum. These seminal books
seem dated today. In 1967 the World Council of Churches
published a study subtitled: 'A Quest for Structures for
Missionary Congregations'. The quest continues.

Management necessarily involves the psychological and
sociological phenomena to do with motivation, influence,
competition, group dynamics, ideological conflict, human
communication, and our need of security. (For a comprehensive account of these issues see Charles Handy's book
Understanding Organizations.[4]) Problematic though they may
be, structures and decisions are necessary for the church to
manage its primary task. When I arrived in Tottenham in
1979 as a vicar it was immediately clear to me (and my new
deaconess colleague) that new structures were needed.
Hitherto decision-making had been greatly dependent on the
vicar. Our hope, by contrast, was that the congregation as a
whole might become much more responsible for the life of the

church. Here is an account of what happened in this particular inner city parish.

Our first move was to start sub-groups of the PCC, each with at least one PCC member serving on it, but thereafter open to *anyone* in the congregation. Soon there were sub-groups concerned with young people, adults' learning, social activities, worship, parish action and 'the world'. The new sub-group structure met with some initial success. Each sub-group worked informally on its chosen area and considerable development took place. The youth group started a Junior Church, a CATS (short for catechumen) group of teenagers and a youth club. They tried to work more closely alongside the Boys Brigade organization. They started a crèche. They raised questions about how it felt to bring children to church, how the children felt, how they could contribute more and fit in better. The adults' learning group started a bookstall. They organized house groups, learning courses, visiting speakers, a more ambitious magazine and links with other churches. The social group noticed the need for black and white people to mix and how the elderly were excluded, and they planned events to meet this situation. Because they had a limited agenda the sub-groups could get further. They attracted people who cared about that particular side of church life. It seemed this was a good way to make progress.

Then morale in the PCC collapsed. Meetings became fractious and boring. It felt as if all the exciting decisions had been made by the sub-groups, and the PCC had become a rubber stamp. When a PCC member wanted to object he or she tended to be told that their point had been considered and 'it would be too complicated to go through all that again here.' What was to be done? The solution was not to return all the power to the PCC, but rather to *develop* its role. The sub-groups were functional. But who was to integrate policies and activities? Were the sub-groups repeating work? What was being left out? What was the over-arching vision? The PCC's role was to attend to these wider questions. Once the problem had been grasped the PCC started to debate major policy issues whose subject matter transcended that of individual sub-groups. Communication became a two way process. The PCC made specific requests of a particular sub-group to carry out a given task on behalf of the church as a whole.

Then a new problem emerged. How could major policy issues about worship, money, pastoral priorities and commitments be discussed by the PCC apart from a more general debate amongst the whole congregation? A structure was needed which would enable the whole congregation to participate. The idea of an open meeting after church was mooted and the pitfalls were listed. It was said that people wouldn't speak, or that they wouldn't stay. It was objected that it would never combine with coffee in the hall, that the children would make a noise, or that it would be chaos. In fact it worked rather well. People felt consulted, and had a space to say what they thought. The PCC began to take the views of those meetings into account. PCC elections for the first time became a live issue in the life of the church. More involvement on the part of more people led to more enthusiasm, confidence and congregational vitality.

No doubt these tentative structures have now changed to meet new situations. The church meeting idea, so fresh at first, has perhaps gone stale. If so, some new design can replace the old. There is nothing sacred about structures.

As the church expanded, so did the volume of work. Agendas grew lengthy, and communications became more difficult. It was decided to breathe life into a defunct 'executive' committee of the PCC to cope with the increased load. The new Executive was efficient. Its membership was small, and it was easy for them to be informed. The fruits of the weekly staff meeting could easily be shared with them. It seemed to be a structure equipped to tackle the most intractable problems. This apparently productive committee, however, began to damage the system. Once again, the PCC was immobilized. The Executive had done the work that counted. The majority of the PCC, after discussion, tended to agree with the decision of the Executive. The opposition, feeling undermined, tended to remain silent. The result was that the actual opposition was only made manifest later by half-hearted effort in the implementation of the decisions. Fortunately the problem was again identified. The Executive changed its role. It began to give major attention to the

question 'What preparation will best enable the next PCC to
have a well-informed and considered debate?' This was a
correct adjustment. Rather than having all the discussion in
advance the Executive concentrated on facilitating the *rest* of
the PCC to have it. The written agenda might be expanded;
something might be discussed at a full church meeting; PCC
members could be briefed to prepare themselves in some
way, or thought might be given to clarifying the major
arguments in an issue.

This modification in the role of the Executive illustrates
how powerfully a structure influences the organization. The
members of this committee had not changed as people, except
in their openness to an insight about the way they were
working. They were willing to adapt their practice in the light
of its effect. They were willing to look at the process of their
communication, as well as at the formal items of the agenda.

This story of how the management developed at one
particular church happened over several years. It shows how
a church can move from a system of management for
maintenance, depending on the incumbent for almost all
policy, initiative and decisions, to management for *faith
development* which attends both to issues of organizational
efficiency and of associational fellowship. To make *faith
development* the goal of management is entirely appropriate
because the distinctive call of the Church is to be the people
of God. In other words, its primary purpose is to be in a
particular relationship with God and other human beings: its
purpose is *relational* before it is *functional.* No amount of
practical activities alone would fulfil this primary purpose.
The Church is called to *be* something, not just to *do*
something. Its primary task is to receive people from the
parish and relate them through the Church to God (not just
to the church as an organization). This implies planning for
being as well as action, and planning for *people in the parish,*
as well as for events within the organization. This task of
faith development has been described by various analysts
and the following 'five steps' are provided by James D.
Anderson and Ezra Earl Jones.[5]

The first step is the decision, for whatever reason, to enter
the door of the church, or its representative. Then follows a
period of testing out, of deciding whether or not to stay. It is a

time in which hopes of security and meaning begin to be invested in the minister, or the worship, or Scripture, or in members of the congregation. The new member is at this point dependent upon the faith of others. Thirdly comes the decision to participate. The new member finds a unique role within the church and contributes accordingly. Inevitably at some point this stability is challenged by a new anxiety, change or crisis. It might be a disappointment, illness, bereavement or any kind of stress. Fourth comes a second period of testing, which leads one of three ways: to withdrawal, to a reinforcement of dependency or, if all goes well, to the fifth step—the decision to explore faith at a deeper level of self-integration. Which of the three directions is taken depends on what the person feels happens to their invested trust in the church. If their trust is built upon, their anxiety noticed, they may be helped through the present pain and stress to a new level of exploration. But if their trust is broken or not built upon the other two possibilities are more likely.

It is important to emphasize that everyone repeats the whole cycle at each new stage of life. Everyone, in other words, needs to return regularly to a sustaining community. However, the analysis is sufficient to point to the significant difference between a cycle of church life leading to increased dependency and one that leads to realized ministry in the parish and beyond.

The management of faith development in a local congregation will always require two distinct types of management: management of the congregation as an association and organizational management.

Management of the congregation as an association

A church is more than a bureaucracy. Obviously it requires organizational or bureaucratic management, for otherwise the parish secretary could not be paid (or sacked) and the broken lavatory in the church hall could never be mended. But a church congregation is primarily called to interpersonal relationships on an *equal* footing in pursuit of the common goals involved in being the People of God. Associational management is needed to enable the congregation to establish a move towards these common goals.

It is for this reason that we developed PCC sub-groups in Tottenham. Our first concern was not with bureaucratic efficiency but with enabling the church to respond to the profound religious needs of its parishioners. We therefore needed to take account of the actual dynamics of the whole church system, of all that its informal life amounted to, as well as of its formal organizational structures. PCC sub-groups are there to ensure that the church genuinely is a place to belong, that it accepts people as they are, that it welcomes newcomers warmly and that its atmosphere is friendly. Structures are required which promote common associational aims. For example, there needs to be a structure to manage the church's policy about incorporating new members. Some people in the congregation might want to run a course to assist this process. Another group might regard this idea as an offence against personal freedom and spontaneity: the appropriate sub-groups must argue this out before a decision can be made. Associational management aims to provide a sound fit between the needs and aspirations of parishioners and the conventions, behaviour and resources of church life. Do their hopes, for example, fit the goals of the currently elected PCC? Are there adequate structures to help people learn, grow in prayer and participate in worship? Is there a means by which I can make my own needs felt or a programme by which I can help others? Does the church meet human needs within the parish? It is the role of the PCC with its sub-groups (or whatever other structures are chosen) to ensure that proper connections are made.

We have seen so far how PCC sub-groups in Tottenham made these connections. Any type of parish can develop this style of management, even those whose commitment to traditional structures is as strong as that of my caricature of *The Parish Church* in Chapter Three. Often a change of incumbent will provide the stimulus to a new approach. When Canon Pumpkin retired from *The Parish Church*, the bishop appointed a dynamic young rector from Scotland called Mr McTalent. Now after two years as rector Mr McTalent preaches a visionary sermon in which he outlines his hopes for the church's future. He says:

Were the parish consulted? ah!

When I look at what we spend our time and money on and compare it with what the parish really needs from us, I sense a sad mismatch between them. In the coming weeks, I want us to share together *your* sense of what we *are* doing and what we *should be* doing . . .

The congregation duly compiles its response. The analysis of all the data shows that the church at the moment only meets the needs of those who enjoy its activities, as if it is a kind of club. The data also show a desire on the part of many people to serve the parish, especially the notorious Arcadia Estate, if only they can see a way of being able to do this. They begin to see that unless drastic change is introduced by themselves, the introverted life of the Parish Church will continue indefinitely. As they go on discussing their dilemma, they realize that what they gain from belonging to the Parish Church does not give them the vision, encouragement and opportunity they need to equip them in the tasks of ministry to the parish. They can now see that if the church *is* to be a means of pastoral care to the people on the Arcadia Estate it needs to learn a new awareness of wounded feelings, such as those which arise from unemployment and racism. If the church *is* to be a community that Arcadia residents will want to belong to, it will need to show involvement in some of their problems, such as housing, inadequate access to public transport and lack of social facilities. If the congregation were to respond imaginatively to *these* issues then people on the Arcadia estate might start to have reason to be interested in the life of the church. The congregation of the Parish Church has at last begun to address the 'mismatch' of Mr McTalent's key sermon.

What the rector does is to encourage his congregation to experience associational management in action. They examine their current performance and compare it with the goals they want to set themselves. They see a marked discrepancy here and come to realize that, while they alone are making demands on their church, they will be unable to achieve their new goals. Once they come to recognize and respond to needs and demands very different from their own, the way is open to them to relate to the residents of the Arcadia estate.

Instead of being a church ghetto meeting its own needs alone, the Parish Church is becoming a church with a ministry of faith development on an inner city housing estate.

Organizational management

Since the church is an inextricable mixture of fellowship and bureaucracy there will inevitably be overlap between associational and organizational management. This second kind of management is required if the newly discovered aspirations of a congregation like Mr McTalent's are to be realized in practice. It includes the management of church plant and fabric, raising the diocesan 'quota' and other funds, communication within and beyond the congregation, secretarial administration and the management of specific projects such as community action or congregational training. There is no single best structure for organizational management of churches. The task is to fit the structure to the situation. It has been likened to that of a tailor who must 'measure the present situation, assess the fit, and perform the necessary alterations'.[6] The need is to be alert, flexible and inventive. Alas, organizational rules in the Church of England are commonly perceived to be permanently fixed, as if inscribed in stone. In fact, as we saw earlier, ministers and congregation are free to ask far-reaching questions about their church structures and to make radical changes if necessary.

The common mistake seems to be to assume too quickly that the clergy are responsible for management, often with disastrous consequences for efficiency. Every member of the congregation has a contribution to make to the leadership and management of their church's ministry. The aim must be that members both feel and are responsible for their church's decisions and structures. Clearly this does not mean that everyone must be involved in every decision. It means rather that they should feel identified with decisions by having participated in their making. There is a marked difference between being on the side that lost the vote and feeling entirely unconsulted.

The adequacy of a church's structures is tellingly revealed by practical details such as the clarity and current accuracy of the notice boards both inside and outside the church. Is the notice board welcoming? Does it say where the church key may be obtained? Does it give information about when and where people may find information from church records? Or, inside the church, is it clear who is responsible for communications? Are there hospitable people at the door with a welcome? Have the sidespeople been properly trained? The efficiency of management may also be detected by how well the church building is used as a vehicle of parish communication. Is it used for the display of school art? Does it house exhibitions such as the history of the local community in photographs? Or is it made available for concerts, drama, community ventures and public meetings? None of these practical events can happen without bureaucratic planning, allocation of roles, suitable training and everything else that goes to make up the business of organizational management.

Particular inner city problems

The inner city setting is not without managerial advantages. Congregations are perhaps less attached to the annual round of unregenerated folk religion (which requires a deeply conservative attitude to church organization) than churches elsewhere. Structural change may be easier to negotiate in Toxteth than in Cumbria. There is also likely to be an openness to what the anthropologist Victor Turner has called *communitas*.[7] By this he means to convey the spontaneous, equally participating relationship experienced, for example, in tribal dancing. In other words there may be a willingness to 'let yourself go' in ways that the tighter behavioural code of other sections of society would hardly permit, but which is congenial to the fostering of a friendly, uninhibited community. This is more than a willingness to dance 'Knees up Mother Brown' or offering hospitality easily. Letting go in this context means being able to adapt to what seems good for your community. Nevertheless there are distinct difficulties. There is evidence that churches set in a turbulent environment such as a neighbourhood in ethnic transition, with fast turnover in housing or with increasing social problems, will tend to decline unless they take steps to accommodate the constant changes around them. The management needed to assimilate new members will always be different from that required to nurture stable ones. But if new members come with different expectations, as they will, the potential for conflict is high. The more varied the congregation becomes the harder it is corporately to agree. The increased need for information will put pressure on the communications system, and this in itself may cause strain and invite conflict. There is no alternative but to build in new expanded structures of communication, and pay attention to the management of conflict. The minister's leadership is of course essential in achieving this.

The question of black people's exclusion from office holding positions in churches cannot be ignored in the inner city. A survey by the Race Relations Commission of the Diocese of Southwark[8] revealed all too clearly the inherent racism at work in some congregations. Where black people are genuinely encouraged to stand for office they do so. This is a demonstrated fact. Where, in a multi-ethnic parish, they are left out, racism is at work. The evidence for this state of affairs is easily revealed. One has only to visit any two parishes, one of which involves black leadership, and compare the attitudes and atmosphere. Black people in one parish are not so different from those in another in the matter of leadership. The truth about the difference will be found not far beneath the surface, in discovering what sort of church the white people in it actually want.

Inner city churches face further managerial difficulties. Its tough, noisy and polluted environment is far from the 'beauty of holiness', usually preferred as an atmosphere for worship. People are troubled; their sense of self-worth tends to be low. Norms within the congregation are not stable and the roles people take up are sometimes, and for good reason, hijacked as a means of satisfying personal needs. Resources are always scarce, and there can easily be a sense that mere survival as an organization is doubtful. For these reasons, even the most meticulously organized and democratically structured congregation stands in need of enthusiastic and visionary leadership, for which it is reasonable for them to look to the minister.

Notes

1. Quoted by H. Küng, *The Church*, Sheed and Ward 1967, p. 441.
2. J. de Blank, *The Parish in Action*, Mowbrays 1959.
3. P. Moore, *The Church Reclaims the City*, SCM 1965.
4. C. Handy, *Understanding Organisations*, Penguin 1986.
5. J. D. Anderson and E. E. Jones, *The Management of Ministry*, New York, Harper and Row 1978, pp. 128 – 131. I am indebted to this book as a whole for the discussion of management and structures in this chapter. See also J. D. Whitehead and E. E. Whitehead, *Method in Ministry*, New York, Seabury 1980.
6. ibid., p. 50.
7. V. Turner, *The Ritual Process*, Aldine 1969.
8. Race Relations Commission of the Diocese of Southwark Survey, 1986.

NINE

The Life and Work of the Inner City Minister

―――――

Again Jesus said, 'The Kingdom of God, what shall I compare it with? It is like yeast which a woman took and mixed with half a hundredweight of flour till it was all leavened.'

Luke 13.20―1

Personal issues

It is five past nine on a Thursday morning, the minister's day off. 'Daddy', calls out his daughter, 'the undertaker's on the phone.' As the minister shuffles into his dressing gown he sees Jack, a familiar homeless wayfarer, coming towards the door to ask for some breakfast. Remaining hopes for his day off are dimmed almost to extinction. It hadn't looked promising. The primary school head had asked him to 'at least look in' because the Education Officer was coming; he had already agreed to accompany Crispin to his court hearing, which could take up most of the morning; and he should never have left writing that article on 'the health emergency' requested by the local paper until today. He feels irritated because he is not normally undisciplined about time off. He knows from experience that it should be sacrosanct. But however much he tries to keep them free some Thursdays are swallowed up with work. It would matter less if the last week had not been so draining. But since last Thursday, there has been vandalism in the church hall, a parish training event, Sunday's services, including baptisms in the afternoon, three funerals, five assorted meetings, fourteen parish visits, two school assemblies, a trip to prison and having the car serviced. Mere details on one level, but they add up to a substantial drain on the emotional resources of one individual.

130

On a rough statistical average this minister's family reckons that something happens in the vicarage about every ten minutes throughout the day. For example, if you take a bath it is likely that, before you are out of it, the doorbell or phone will have rung. Vicarage life seems an endless parade of callers, formal and informal meetings, routines (such as producing the newsletter on Fridays) and unique occurrences. The vicarage atmosphere is often charged with the humour and fun which follows from its prevailing hospitality. The kettle is rarely cold. Unlikely gatherings (the parish secretary, someone who called with some jumble, the homebeat police officer, an unemployed teenager, a tramp and the vicar's visiting aunt from Bournemouth) sit round the big kitchen table for coffee and doughnuts. It is a house accustomed to the violence of angry feelings and acclimatized to tears. It knows break-ins, children's parties and parish rows as well as the steady administrative and pastoral routine. Primarily it is a family home. This dominating purpose sets the tone of everything else. Pastoral care in the vicarage enables the depressed teenager or the man straight out of prison to be received as people rather than clients. Coffee in the vicarage kitchen is far removed from the impersonal coldness of the DHSS area office. As a home, the vicarage offers a quality of response most professional agencies can only envy. The ex-offender, briskly instructed to make coffee for himself and everyone else, takes confidence from this instant inclusion. The invitation to jump into the daily round of an 'open-house' vicarage confers dignity and personhood on visitors. They are not led to feel passive recipients of 'help' but temporary members of a household: people who have something to offer.

Not all inner city vicarages are like this one. Nor should they be, since families differ in their needs, and parishes in their style and resources. But inner city clergy families all face the same issues. The Gallup clergy interview[1] sponsored by *Faith in the City* revealed that clergy in general have a high sense of job satisfaction but that UPA clergy tend to have a *higher* sense of job satisfaction than their colleagues elsewhere. More than half hope to remain in UPAs in their next job. On the other hand clergy exhaustion (or burnout)[2] appears to be twice as serious in UPAs, especially for younger clergy, and younger married clergy in particular (regardless of whether or not their partner is working). Single clergy and church workers, many of whom are women, say that UPAs are more accepting than the suburbs. Homosexual clergy tend to say the same, and that they prefer to work in UPAs because of the accepted diversity of lifestyles. *Faith in the City* reports: 'Many UPA clergy and their wives find it a privilege to bring up their children in a multicultural area.'[3] It is a setting of both opportunities and snags. Language can be a significant barrier in an Asian area. The middle-class social background of most clergy and their partners finds expression in the number (32%) who send their children to fee-paying secondary schools. Against this, some clergy have a positive experience of educating their children in local schools. When the present Bishop of New York was serving in the slums of Jersey City in the 1950s his children were sent to the neighbourhood school because he and his wife believed it would help teach them how to live. It might have been expected that their academic progress would be inhibited as a result, but it turned out that when the eldest child was tested at a leading New York City private school after two years she had achieved as much as her Manhattan peers in most areas of study and was ahead of them in some!

The demands upon an inner city vicarage will be considerable. A couple or family can begin to feel they live their lives in public. They may find themselves rowing in front of others or burying family conflict altogether until breakdown threatens. There may be pressure on rooms as family and parish compete for their use. There may be a sense of intrusion both physically and emotionally. It may feel that the minister, though physically present, is being eaten up by an omnivorous parish, and that he or she is never really available. Hours of work may be long. Sharp criticism of the minister may be heard, even within the vicarage. Communications may break down. Perhaps the family are not consulted about parish plans which will affect them. It may feel impossible to stop the flow of demand when the moment comes for time off. There may be fear of the environment: of mugging, violence or rape. Last, but not unimportant, it may be hard or impossible to claim legitimate expenses from a church that is struggling to survive. These are the snags which must be squarely admitted. Some families could not responsibly consider ministry in a UPA in their particular circumstances. Others may try but find it necessary to leave after a short time or a few years. If so they will have made a perfectly valid contribution. Many clergy families will thrive in a UPA.

Inner city ministry requires robustness rather than heroism. Its disadvantages can be faced and to a certain extent met. Ministers and their families, to survive, must learn how to say 'no'. Ministers are not omnipotent. This fantasy is dangerous for the minister and unhelpful to the parishioner, as well as for the mental health of family life. Time off, adequate holidays and proper timetabling for the family in suitable privacy are as essential as food and sleep. For many clergy families in the inner city, crucial though it is to keep work within limits, there will be a fundamental compatability between parish and family life. The advantages will outweigh the disadvantages. I had already been a vicar in Tottenham for three years when I got married. Our fantasy and anxiety was that we would never have time for ourselves, that the parish would make unreasonable demands on married life and that it would be hard for my wife (who had a full-time job) to retain her independence in the face of congregational expectations. Our experience was humbling. Cathy was greatly taken by surprise to discover the warmth, encouragement, support and friendship which opened up to her. She found the open *ambience* of the vicarage enriching. When our daughter arrived she was surrounded with support (not to mention soft toys). When the parish mounted a play and for a week the vicarage took on the life of the back stage of a playhouse she found herself involved and delighted rather than resentful. The development of the life of the church, often an exciting enterprise, complemented our development as a family. This compatibility of the professional and the personal can also be experienced in the work. The team of ministers whether clerical or lay, support each other as they pray the Office together or take time each day for a staff meeting. This is especially important for single clergy. A quick sherry after Evensong affords the opportunity to talk through the day, to share any difficult or painful encounters or anxiety, and to resolve any niggling conflict. It is easy to

How very middle
— class!

make deep attachments and friendships in a UPA. So it is not surprising that many clergy and their families experience a tearing grief when the time comes to move on. It can hardly be done without leaving a part of themselves behind.

The minister's work

The vision of a congregation will not for long outflank that of its ministers. The ambitions of a congregation tailor themselves to his or her ministerial expectations. This means the minister holds considerable power. He or she carries a decisive responsibility for the vision of the gospel that congregation puts into practice. However, the art of the minister depends on making his or her views known in such a way that those who oppose them are given plenty of space and encouragement. It is possible to create an atmosphere in which differing styles, commitments, interpretations and priorities coexist in the mutual knowledge that no one is ever wholly right and everyone has something to learn from the other side. This atmosphere of unity in diversity matters greatly in parish pastoral care. To achieve such breadth and tolerance in community is one of the minister's top priorities.

Bill is a minister who has failed to understand this. He arrived six months ago as priest-in-charge of a UPA parish. Bill's central concern is justice. He is determined to transform the approach to Christianity he finds in the congregation which he sees as racially prejudiced and politically conservative. For example, the congregation are opposed to his desire to affiliate the church to the local 'Police Monitoring Committee' set up to investigate allegations of police brutality. For Bill the issue of justice is paramount. He believes that a church which cannot take a stand on issues of justice should be closed. He has therefore preached and spoken about little else since his arrival. Bill's effect on the congregation has been drastic, but it has not inspired a renewed commitment to justice. It has merely depleted the average attendance from eighty-seven to twenty-six. Bill feels rejected. He is angry at the congregation's refusal to take the claims of faith seriously. But he fails to see how angry the congregation is with him. They feel he does not appreciate what to them is of greatest value in the life of the church. He has not established a basis of trust between them. He has not preached his vision from within a framework of sound human relationships but in place of it. Yet the rightness of a cause is no replacement for pastoral care. Bill needs help to learn the necessary interdependence of pastoral and prophetic ministry. The point is a practical one: Bill's righteous anger may be justified, but it is not effective as leadership.

Congregations may feel that the limitations of a minister's temperament and pastoral ability curtail the tolerance and diversity of church life. If so it is important not to shy away from struggling with the question of how to help him or her become more open. What lies behind the attitudes which seem to block rather than nurture congregational growth? The minister may feel embattled or defeated. Of course the issue of clergy support and continued training is one for the wider church institution. Regular talks with someone in the church hierarchy are essential, as is the opportunity to work with a personal consultant and access to further study. But the congregation is also an important resource for the nurture of the minister. It is sad when a congregation feels itself rendered impotent by the defensiveness of the vicar, yet this is not uncommon. Where it occurs the formal and informal congregational leadership has the difficult task of considering how to respond. But respond they must. A minister who has become bitter, taken to drink, withdrawn into the vicarage or who lives on the edge of despair needs to be actively cared for rather than written off.

The minister holds a key position. There will be a close connection between what he or she stands for and what the church is seen to stand for. The minister is experienced as a unifying focus at the centre, but he or she also holds the boundaries. What has been said about the importance of diversity refers to inevitable temperamental differences between people. The scope of these routine differences is broad. It includes the places where people feel hurt by each other, left out, annoyed and most of the emotional turbulence of parish life. But there are limits, and the minister has responsibility for them. From time to time the parish can expect to witness a serious breaking of boundaries such as those which occur in family breakdown, sexual infidelity, misconduct at work, or criminal delinquency. The minister's role when boundaries are broken, is not to set up as a kind of parish prosecutor but to help those concerned to face their situation as it is. There is no room for exaggerated or reflex responses such as revenge, total condemnation, smugness or instant rejection. Feelings may be expected to run high and if they are to be expressed but contained the minister involved may have a role in the creation of safe situations in which necessary but controlled exchanges between the various parties can take place. The aim is to help those involved connect the church's pastoral experience of this problem wisely to their own particular situation. It is important not to confuse delinquency with sub-christian quirks of personality and background conditioning which hardly amount to a considered bid to dismantle the values of the church, as some individual members of the congregation might appear to believe. Every day ministers hear of Mary's determination never to forgive Betty, and of George's refusal to speak to Arthur ever again. These incidents offend the spirit of the gospel, but such offensiveness is rarely translated into a resolution of the PCC.

1. *Leading from the front: the responsibility for mission*

The minister is a missioner. He or she holds responsibility (with, as in all ministry, the bishop) for evangelism in the parish. This means leading from the front. In preaching, writing, talking, work in groups, public stance and by the model of their own life and example, ministers proclaim, explain and encourage their vision of the gospel and its meaning for every particular of parish life. This leading from the front will affect every department of church life: the style of worship, the church's stand on local (or wider) issues, the quality of the congregation's community life, the activities and projects undertaken by the church, the organizational structures—all these will be strongly influenced by the minister's lead. The importance of sharing power does not eliminate the ministers' central role in developing the life of the church according to their understanding of the gospel. That is their job. That is part of their authorization. If ministers do not lead with their own theological vision

someone unauthorized will soon attempt to usurp their
authority. It is partly to safeguard the orthodoxy of the gospel
in its parish proclamation and style of living that the church
ordains ministers in the first place. The crucial distinction is
between responsibility for a vision of church life and
autocratic rule to achieve that vision. The Kingdom is not
served by bossy vicars. It is one thing to preach what they
believe — that is what ministers are there for. It is quite
another, and a disaster, to use ministerial power to force
views on the church's decisions. The reason for this is,
obviously, that a paternalistic, authoritarian style of leadership is incompatible with the quality of corporate life implied
by the gospel. It is a contradiction in terms for a congregation
to 'own' its faith and worship, to be growing in interdependent
pastoral care and confidence, to be taking responsibility for
the implications of the gospel *and* to be submissively
dependent for all decisions on the minister. Some clergy seem
to be unable to grasp the important distinction between
authority rightly held and exercised, we might call it the
authority to preach, and the authority of an omnipotent
managing director. They seem to think you can't have one
without the other. You can. Without a grasp of this distinction
ministers will be of little use at the next, and equally central,
dimension of their work.

2. *Leading from behind: the responsibility
   to enable*

The enabling/facilitating role of the minister is far too
important for the charges of 'jargon' to be allowed to stick.
Enabling or facilitating refers to the creative and costly work
of assisting others to grow into their own maturity and
potential. In a church this has both an individual and a
corporate reference since for Christians human growth is not
just about the blossoming of individuals for their own sake. It
is also about the formation of mature communities to
accomplish the tasks of the gospel. The minister therefore
needs to give as much time and attention to the fostering of
groups and the relations between them as to individuals. As
enablers, ministers do not rush in with their own views. They
listen and attend to what is said in many meetings where

ideas are expressed or decisions taken with which they disagree.

I would like to illustrate this by mentioning an evening group which took place early on in my time as a vicar in Tottenham. The subject was 'How we imagine Jesus'. I invited the members of the group to say frankly what they thought and believed about Jesus. I found myself working hard to help people say what they really felt rather than automatically describing what they thought they ought to say or what they remembered from Sunday School. It was in some ways a painful evening. When the truth emerged people admitted that what they believed had little resemblance to Christian orthodoxy. (They were all long-standing church members.) The picture we drew up of Jesus that evening was completely doubtful as history or orthodoxy. But it was a significant step forward in faith for those people. There was the act of honest sharing; the valued picture of a Jesus who really *meant* something to them; the discovery that others were similarly confused; the recognition of theological ignorance — that all they had were childhood images built into adult life; the prayers at the end in which I mentioned the qualities of Jesus they had named. All these ingredients made for an evening of growth and disclosure on which they were subsequently able to build. My ministerial responsibility that evening was to enable the group to have the confidence to express themselves. It would have been all too easy for them to have fallen into the trap of asking me to give them the answers as 'the one who ought to know'. I was more useful by not letting the 'right answers' freeze up what seemed to me an inspired experience of learning.

Much of the enabling role is summed up in the word 'support'. In an inner city church people *will* read in church, do the intercessions, even preach. They *will* run this group, visit this person, apply for this grant. They *will* hold office and take this responsibility. But they will need support. This means they will need preliminary encouragement. It is a fantasy to imagine that a majority of people will spontaneously offer, say, to lead the intercessions in church. A general invitation will not be responded to by more than a few. But a judicious phone call or better, a visit to suggest this, will often have a quite different effect. There is pleasure in being personally approached. It implies the person is valued, and that the minister believes this to be a task the person can do. The suggestion is likely to be met with diffidence so that sensitivity is needed to discern whether encouragement or withdrawal is appropriate. Often a mild encouragement together with the offer of assistance in preparation and a rehearsal in church will result in an affirmative answer.

Support involves not just initial enthusiasm but continued care. Perhaps a woman parishioner has agreed to lead the intercessions but now feels apprehensive. She may regret the decision, or feel ambivalent about it. To support her is to be aware of how she feels and to provide sufficient room for her to express it. By talking over her anxieties it may be possible for her to feel relieved of them. Then on the day she is to lead the prayers, support is again important both in ensuring she feels prepared, and in arranging practicalities. The custom of some churches of gathering all those with responsibilities for leading worship for a vestry prayer may be helpful, as may enlisting the support of the congregation by thanking her for her prayers during the notices. If gently accomplished these details do not detract from the devotions themselves, they enhance them. Finally it is a part of support to thank her after the service, talk through her feelings about it and any implications for the future.

Support like this can make all the difference to how people feel. It is what is meant here by leading from behind. I have seen people change from being diffident, apparently inarticulate and irresponsible, to becoming confident, talkative, assertive and competent as a result of church encouragement and support. And I have seen this occur even when the circumstance which introduced them to the church was a disaster like unemployment, a hospital operation or bereavement. Groups need a similar support. It is no good asking a small group to take on a community project and leaving them to it. They will easily fall victim to internal wrangling or external pressure. To secure the confidence to *work through* problems as they arise the group will need sensitive facilitation and warm encouragement, a theme developed in the next chapter.

3. *The Church's ambassador to the parish*

As school children are told they 'represent' the school on the bus home, so all Christians always represent the Church. But the minister's ambassadorial role is distinctive. Ambassadors do not *replace* the government of a country. They represent it in a publicly recognized fashion. Customs, symbols, jokes, advantages and limitations cluster round this representation. The office transcends the person. It is not because the Reverend John Jones goes into the pub that someone starts to tell him why they don't go to church, it's because he's the Reverend 'The Curate.' As the public representative of the church, recognizable by clothing, and usually living 'over the shop' the minister has unique opportunities. The church is the only agency in a UPA to have professional staff who both work and *live* in every parish.

The involvement, knowledge and flexibility of the clergy and other professional church workers enables them to build bridges between agencies, and between agencies and local people. In Tottenham, for example, the churches were responsible for setting up a bimonthly multi-agency lunch to which representatives of both statutory and voluntary agencies came, as well as local residents. This became a useful opportunity that would not otherwise have existed for inter-disciplinary discussion, sharing of common problems, corporate action and, most important, getting to know other workers involved in the same area. The liberty to set up a multi-agency lunch meeting is an example of how useful the professional freedom of the clergy can be. Unrestricted by the tight legislation of their social work colleagues, for example, clergy can respond to needs flexibly, using their experience of living on the spot. It did not take me very long in Tottenham to see that health visitors did not know home beat officers, social workers did not know teachers and GPs did not, on the whole, know anyone at all. Only the clergy were in a position to do something about this professional isolation. Equally when other agencies are empty and shut—in the evenings, at weekends or on public holidays—the clergy are still available. The Social Services Department in Tottenham, for example, rang me every year to discuss how the church could help over Christmas.

The minister does have, as a matter of fact, more contact as a *Christian* than other members of the church with parishioners in general through the continual round of funerals, baptisms, marriages, school assemblies, committee meetings, hospital visits and professional support of local institutions and agencies. It is the minister who is asked to write up the church's view on the proposed sex shop in the parish for the local paper not the churchwarden. It is the minister who is rarely able to buy the drinks in a neighbourhood pub. And it is to the vicarage that the merry-go-round of jumble salers, wayfarers who suddenly need to visit their 'uncle in Birmingham,' and other needy people first go.

The minister's key position makes it possible for his or her diary to be filled up many times over. The minister is in contact with thousands of people, large numbers of whom as individuals would appreciate some time spent with them. In a crisis time, during the later stages of a terminal illness, for example, or following the death of someone well known to the minister, hours each day can be spent concerned with just one family, say, if the sick person is in a hospital some miles away and has a young family who need support at home. Church groups, a parish school, the fostering of even *one* particular project (be it for the unemployed or the restoration of the church roof), the slow building of credible relationships with local agencies, preparing worship, supporting colleagues and church office holders, taking funerals (eight a week or more are possible in a large inner city parish) and visiting before and after the service, making time for young people and children, some time for counselling, reading and study . . . it is an endless list. Inner city ministers can easily find themselves working a hundred-hour week.

There is no easy answer as to how to get the balance right. The critical steering is between predetermined tasks which are necessary for the building up of the life of the church, and sufficient space to remain responsive to events and needs as they arise. If *all* a minister's time is given to a diaried schedule of prearranged priorities it will ignore the ministerial priority to be somewhat available. But it is easy to be swamped by the progress of the day. If someone calls at the front door in some kind of need it cannot always be right to fend them off with the excuse that this is the morning you had set aside to catch up on the parish card index! But despite the grave difficulties of keeping a balance, the minister's ability to *control* how much of their time is spent, the inbuilt flexibility of the job, is a privilege. Given good discipline and a certain experience it can be managed to advantage. Pastorally the issue turns on whether or not ministers are in touch with the needs in themselves that are being met by their work. What is meant by this is illustrated in the next chapter as it is an issue inevitably brought to light when a minister leads a group (see pp. 154—6). Some ministers deny the existence of their own needs. Putting down all their work to the call of the gospel they overwork to the point of illness. Such ministers need help to become aware of their own compulsions and so learn to switch off the part of them which, unacknowledged, would have them do *another* two visits before bedtime without pausing to consider the consequences for their own physical and mental well being.

4. *A leader in prayer*

All men and women are called into relationship with God. Ministers are called to be catalysts helping this relationship to grow. Everything a minister says and does is suffused with this purpose. If the minister's actions are the making of a painting, prayer is the paint being used. Prayer and person belong together like light in glass. Without prayer a minister's work loses its breath. Everything a church is about is directed towards God: it is for his glory, in his praise and all in thanksgiving for and in response to his love. Any role the minister has in leading public worship, celebrating the sacraments, visiting with holy communion or otherwise explicitly officiating in prayer is set within this wider vocation. It is this call to facilitate the religious life of those in their care that sets a minister apart, not some specific sacerdotal function within it. It is a role shared by all Christians in their ministry to others. For example, those who have trained to take part in a parish pastoral care scheme will presumably have been helped to learn how to pray with those they visit wherever this is appropriate. Ministers do not have any exclusive rights as a catalyst, but their whole work is directed to this end. They have been especially trained, authorized and if necessary given a stipend to set them free in this particular task. It means, clearly, that ministers have a vocation as men and women of prayer. Only the person whose own life is rooted in prayer can help others to pray. Only those who pray through their own anxieties, weaknesses, compulsions and agnosticism can be the exemplary sacrament others need to help them do the same. Only those who themselves find words for God from their own agony can find prayers to express the agony of those in their care. And only those who listen contemplatively to the silent mystery of God's voice will be able to inspire others to meditate upon God's love for them.

However emphatic the congregation's role in it, the minister rightly plays a central and creative part in the celebration of the liturgy. It is not true that style is of no importance, or of only negative importance in so far as it focuses attention on the celebrant rather than on God. A droned incantation does not draw attention to God; it interferes with the effective communication of the liturgy's meaning. And to celebrate the liturgy with an inflection that does justice to the sentiment of the words spoken is no more than natural. If it is in the personality of the minister to dramatize, sentimentalize or exaggerate the piety of what is being said of course this will communicate itself to those who hear. But so will an attempt to cloak the personality behind some kind of priestly verbal veil, to drop a liturgical equivalent of the screen used in theatres before the entry of a ghost. The minister as celebrant sets the pace, creates the spaces, and decisively animates the atmosphere of the liturgy. The style will be telling—an indication of the spiritual temperature of the worship. To celebrate is to strike the tone of the worship on behalf of the congregation, not an opportunity for celebrants to express their liturgical tastes or dramatic talent as if they were performing a soliloquy.

The image of celebrants standing at the centre of things whilst saying words which point away from themselves illustrates well the paradox of their status in the context of this book. They are the prime enablers of parish pastoral care. Their leadership is indispensable, but only as that of a servant.

[handwritten annotation: └ 4 whom?]

Notes

1. *Faith in the City*, p. 32f. and pp. 129–34.
2. See J. A. Sanford, *Ministry Burnout*, Arthur James 1984.
3. *Faith in the City*, p. 131.

[handwritten annotation: I find this somewhat clericalist and rather contradicts previous ch.]

TEN

Use of the Small Group

'For where two or three are gathered in my name, there
am I in the midst of them.'

Matt. 18.20

The most versatile and creative structure for the animation of
church life is the small group. This is true for the church
anywhere so that much of this chapter is generally applicable
rather than confined to the inner city in its relevance.
However, the inner city situation requires that small groups
be used appropriately to meet the needs of those who live
there. So this chapter will also seek to relate the use of the
small group specifically to the inner city setting.

In order to understand what is happening in a small group
it is usual and useful to distinguish between *content* and
process. The *content* refers to the meeting as it would be
known from a transcript of everything said. *Hansard* gives
an account of the *content* of House of Commons debates. The
process refers to the rest of what is 'going on' but which
would not appear on a transcript. For example, if I say 'I'm
not angry' in a high-pitched scream, through clenched teeth
and with a reddening face, only the words 'I'm not angry' will
appear on the transcript. They are the content. The
accompanying responses belong to the process. The process
includes *how* things are said, what people look like when
they are speaking, how and where they are sitting and what
they are feeling. As in the example just given, content and
process can often be at variance.

Not all the process is observable, though some of it is,
enabling such observations as who speaks most, who remains
quiet, who allies with whom, what gestures are made, the
way people sit and who sits next to whom. The unobservable

part consists of what remains inside people: what is going on in their minds and how they feel. It includes their attitudes and assumptions. This level will only be known if individuals share something of it with the group.

Most formal education is primarily concerned with the level of content. It is common for groups to consider nothing else. The PCC argument about a child care group using the church hall would appear from the minutes to have been entirely about money, a question of whether or not they could afford the rent. Those who opposed the idea became so drawn into the content of the discussion of finances they failed to register the true cause of their opposition, namely, resentment that the last group to use the hall always left it untidy. The content is seductive in this way. It is easy to become so caught up in its detail that a discussion proceeds which is deaf to the realities of the process beneath it. The importance of this distinction is that from a pastoral point of view a group's content can never be considered in isolation from its process. A person's contribution to the discussion will be affected by all that makes up their inner world. For example in the Lent Group whose members discussed their idea of Jesus (described in the last chapter) each person's contribution was determined not only by their formal education but the attitudes, feelings and particular puzzling unique to his or her story. Moreover, though I did not discuss this in the last chapter, the interaction of group members must always be taken account of in order to understand the relationship between the content and process of the group. As we shall see in this chapter (pp. 150–4), to understand the small group's process the pastor must bear in mind not only the differing inner worlds of individual group members but the dynamics that arise between them. Had I as a pastor responded to the group only on the level of content, say, taking on the role of an historical scholar concerned to establish facts about Jesus and to dispute dubious historical ideas about him, I would entirely have failed to utilize the group's inherent opportunity for personal growth.

The significance of small groups for an inner city parish is that they provide a structure which, by attending to the process as well as the content, can act as scaffolding between the dereliction of inner city life and the wholeness of relief from anger, grief or depression. Belonging to a small group can lead to new confidence, healing and growth. All the preceding chapters of Parts 2 and 3 presuppose the utilization of small groups in the life of the church to realize their particular concerns. Thus worship is prepared in small groups, learning takes place in small groups, healing occurs in the sharing and support made possible by the small group, and small groups can kindle acts of service. Something of all these features can be illustrated by part of a joint sermon given by a group of women from the congregation of the Tottenham church of which I was vicar. The group consisted of five women. Two worked as housewives, two were cleaners and one a seamstress. They met weekly during an Advent season. It must be said that the group was lucky in finding itself able to ride through the often rough waters of small group dynamics without capsizing, particularly as no leader was appointed, though written guidelines were supplied which provided a firm structure for each meeting. No doubt members of the group *did* experience difficulties during group sessions. But from their own account of it we can infer that it was their ability to share with one another, already noted as a frequently met positive characteristic of UPA culture, and their willingness to listen to each other, which enabled them to steer through the problems so commonly encountered in small groups and which this chapter is concerned to describe and consider (pp. 150ff.). Whatever the cause of their fortune, this group found their Advent meetings for prayer, silence and discussion of biblical readings to be a confidence-building and enriching experience, one which they subsequently shared with the whole congregation in a sermon from which these extracts are taken:

Lindy
Can I tell you that our group was very special to me. The girls taught me a lot. The group made me happy and I felt joy and love. I wasn't afraid of being myself, and I had a great feeling of belonging. Our friendship grew through God's love.

Clare
I felt a closeness with the others. After a couple of weeks I didn't mind saying what I felt without wondering if the

others would think I was daft. Praying aloud became a bit easier, not a lot (*laughter*), but we were all the same, none of us had much practice before. I felt closer to God during our prayers together than during prayers at church. I don't know why. Perhaps the distractions were less, perhaps the prayers were simpler for us all to understand. It was nice to get other people's ideas on the Bible readings. It makes it easier to understand when there are a few views.

Doris
The group gave me a feeling of warmth, friendship and confidence. Also a deeper understanding of the Bible through other people's interpretations. Over the weeks I became more at ease and was able to say more about what I felt. The highlight was the Senior Citizens Christmas Party, which gave a feeling of a job well done.

Betty
To me the groups meant:
Firstly, love, friendship and confidence to say what I felt without feeling foolish. Secondly, the Bible readings — which we took in turns in reading aloud and discussing afterwards, were made clearer. Lastly, we had some lovely lunches together and I'm looking forward to the group starting again, when I'm sure we should learn even more now we've got over any initial shyness we all felt at the beginning of the group meetings.

Marion
To me the group gave a feeling of belonging and friendship. A sense of confidence in being able to discuss the Bible readings without feeling foolish and in giving the senior citizens their Christmas party. Well, it just gave a touch of usefulness and achievement.

The mention of a senior citizens Christmas party refers to the group's decision to express itself in action. They organized, raised funds, catered for, and hosted a Christmas party including a sit-down meal for some forty senior citizens in the church hall. This illustration shows the power of one modest Advent Group to affect deeply the lives of five inner city people.

Groups, however, are *not* a panacea for the social and

psychological bruising of a UPA environment. Their undoubted potential must be balanced both by a realistic understanding of their usefulness and an awareness of group process and its pitfalls. Hope placed in the possibilities of small group membership must take fundamental account of the universal *ambivalence* felt by human beings towards belonging. Of course we need to belong. No one wants to feel lonely and isolated. But we fear the loss of the separateness which confers our personal identity. Which is why the sense that groups are dreadful is also never far away. There is an immense literature on the subject of groups and group process.[1] The concern of this chapter is simply to note some of the basic features of a church-based group and, in particular, the main pastoral considerations in leading such a group.

An idea which I believe should be resisted is the class-related notion that working-class people do not feel comfortable in small groups; that groups are essentially a middle-class activity. This seems to me to be nonsense. *All* human beings feel ambiguous about belonging to a group. While there is a recognizable working-class diffidence about attempting to articulate abstract ideas and theoretical discussion, this is not the same as a working-class diffidence towards group membership as such. But this is a commonly expressed view, not least by middle-class people who perhaps have no ability to imagine a group other than one to discuss issues in a middle-class way. But to jump from that limited view to the conclusion that working-class parishioners cannot benefit from groups is a mistake. Clergy who say so perhaps reflect their own anxiety more than sociological perception. I feel this strongly as I believe the underdevelopment of well organized small groups to be the single most significant factor in the inhibition of lively inner city congregations. No wonder the parish church is moribund, when all you have is an eccentric parson and a collection of scattered individuals, however sincere or well-intentioned. So while small groups are not a magic cure of all ills, and certainly not an *automatic* recipe for church growth I would argue that unless a congregation has a considered strategy for the development and use of small groups it is very unlikely to be a successful agent of pastoral care in the surrounding parish.

My own experience would endorse it.

What, then, needs to be thought about in relation to groups
and how they work? This question can be considered under
two headings; dynamics and leadership.

1.   Group Dynamics: a basic description

An inner city church small group is aiming for two separate
results: the building up of persons in what R. A. Lambourne
called 'we-formation'[2] as a Christian fellowship in the
service of God's Kingdom, and the achievement of practical
tasks, also in the service of God's Kingdom. However, though
distinct, these two purposes belong together. There is no task
in the service of God's Kingdom which is not also concerned
at some level, however far removed, with the building up of
persons. Thus even a group convened to organize the window
cleaning is still a group of people with needs and feelings.
And every group has a practical task even if, like a therapy
group, it is expressly convened to build up persons (i.e. in
this group the task is therapy!). Groups, then, are always
simultaneously person-related and task-related. The human
needs go grinding on whatever the task of the group is
supposed to be.

The theory of group dynamics is concerned to point to the
ways in which the task of the group may be obstructed by
unconscious processes occurring within it. Any group gains
an unconscious life of its own and tends to follow certain
patterns into which all its members are unwittingly drawn.
The work of Wilfred Bion postulates three 'basic assumptions'
a group can unconsciously make as a defence against anxiety.
Each 'basic assumption' has the unconscious aim of trying to
make the situation safe. But when these 'basic assumptions'
remain undetected they may result in the failure of the group
to achieve its intended task. Bion mentions

Dependency
Pairing
Fight/flight

The group will make only one of the three assumptions at
once (though it can change assumptions during a meeting).

(a) *Dependency*

Bion says that a group makes the basic assumption of dependency when it behaves as if 'the group is met in order to be sustained by a leader on whom it depends for nourishment, material and spiritual, and protection.' This results in members of the group being immobilized by a sense of inadequacy, and a quite inflated expectation of the leader. So when a church council finds itself expecting the vicar to be all-powerful, and when normally competent individuals shrink into diffidence, or when members find themselves behaving like children then this basic assumption may be getting the upper hand.

(b) *Pairing*

Bion's second 'basic assumption', pairing, stems from his observation that group sessions can be dominated by two people alone. The rest of the group sometimes seem content to lay aside their own initiative, leaving it all to this couple. Perhaps everyone on the PCC is known to feel strongly for or against a particular response to marijuana-smoking in the youth club, but in the meeting they say nothing, leaving the passionate argument to be had by two people alone. Or perhaps two members of the planning committee corner all the initiative concerning the building project despite the fact that, on a rational level, other members of the group disagree. Bion observed that the group seemed unconsciously to be investing their *hope,* (perhaps to be free from their own fears) in the pair. It is as if there is no need for the others to worry, provided the pair carry the group's future between them. By an unconscious investment of hope in the pair the group shields itself from facing up to deeper levels of fear, conflict or depression that its members might otherwise notice. The pair who outwardly appear to be working creatively on behalf of the group are actually being used to deal with its anxiety.

(c) *Fight/flight*

The third basic assumption Bion notices is that 'the group has met to fight something or to run away from it.' The fight/flight assumption presupposes a split in which 'badness' and 'threat' are kept safely *outside* the group as they concentrate on the business of fighting or running away from

it. A neat, but paranoid, solution to the problem they in fact
have of facing up to hostility and anxiety *within* the group.
The snags are obvious. You can't be working to build up the
parish pastoral care scheme if you spend all the group time
attacking the bishop or wondering how to avoid the
archdeacon.

Before considering what helps to maintain the group as a
work group, or in other words helps it to accomplish a
designated task, we should note how the *development* of a
group, as well as its basic assumptions, influences the
dynamics of its process. The most common titles[3] for the
developing phases of a group's cycle are the stages:

   (i)   Forming
   (ii) Storming
   (iii) Norming
   (iv) Performing

(i) *Forming*
At the beginning of a group, individual members are asking
themselves:

   'who am I in this group?'
   'will I have any control over what goes on?'
   'will there be anything in it for me?'
   'will I be liked?'
   'will the group get too intimate for me?'

In response to this inner questioning some individuals will
assert themselves, maybe aggressively. Others will be meeker.
They will seek out those who might support them, make
alliances and thereafter avoid, or attempt to mollify, any hint
of conflict or aggression. Still others will deny having any
needs or feelings themselves and adopt a withdrawn position
often claimed (falsely) to be based on rationality alone. At
this stage a group needs to discuss its purpose, its name, its
terms of reference, the limits of its membership, its leadership
and its lifespan.

(ii) *Storming*
In the forming stage the anxiety for acceptance often produces
solutions or agreements which turn out to be less than a real
consensus. Storming occurs when sufficient confidence and

identity have been established to permit some conflict. The initial conclusions reached about the group's aims, leadership or procedures are challenged as individuals reveal their more deep personal agendas.

Charlie, who in the first meeting had said how happy he was that the group had been formed, admits in the second meeting how annoyed he had been that the leader had let the group sit in silence instead of explaining what he wanted the group to do. Mary follows this by declaring her irritation with Charlie for being late. Fred points out that the first group had not been what he really expected or hoped for, and so on.

This stage may be characterized by some hostility between members which will need to be contained by the group with the help of the leader. However, resolution of the storming stage should lead to a more genuine trust and more realistic aims than were originally established.

(iii) *Norming*

In this stage the group discovers what it is going to take as normative in the way it works and the way its members relate. This happens by members of the group testing out their own behaviour on the group. It refers to the stage when group members sense the viability of the group. They take on new roles and feel sufficiently confident to express their personal opinions and more intimate feelings. Mary says: 'First I didn't know what to make of you, Charlie. Then, if I'm honest, I thought you were a loudmouth and a show-off. But now I can see that you help us all to look at what we are really feeling. You don't let us settle for the easy way out of just being nice to each other. Thank you, Charlie.' As 'norming' occurs in this way the group establishes its boundaries, ways of making decisions and its depth of openness and trust.

(iv) *Performing*

This stage is reached when the previous three have been successfully worked through. It refers to the stage in which the group is working at its optimum capacity or has reached its full maturity. Obviously groups will in a sense have been 'performing' all along. A 'performing' group is one that has moved beyond individual bids for attention or leadership and other features of a developing group. In practice the chances of a group remaining in this stage are slim and problems from the developing stages can be expected to recur.

2.   Group Leadership: the pastoral skills needed

Group dynamics do not operate like a machine inexorably producing identical results and permitting no change once the design has been fixed and the apparatus switched on. Neither are they a capricious, ghostly presence manipulating the group like gods in a Nordic myth. Any mystique surrounding group dynamics should be dispelled. As far as group dynamics are concerned the pastor's job is, as the British Passport has it, to allow the group to pass freely without let or hindrance and to afford the group such assistance and protection as may be necessary.

This does *not* require specialist knowledge, psychotherapeutic qualifications or unusual skills. It *does* require:

(a) appropriate self-knowledge;
(b) generalist pastoral skills;
(c) a willingness to accept certain responsibilities;
(d) a basic understanding of how groups work;
(e) clarity of group purpose;

together with, of course, the ability to *apply* all this within the live group session.

(a) *Appropriate self-knowledge*
A diagram may be helpful here:

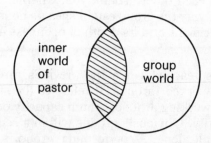

In the above figure, the left-hand circle represents the inner world of the pastor. The right-hand circle represents the whole world of the group, including the inner worlds of all its members with their feelings and assumptions. The shaded area in the middle is that area where the inner world of the pastor properly overlaps with the group world. In other words the group world *impinges* on the inner world of the pastor. In so far as it does, the pastor's contribution to the group will be influenced by his or her own inner needs. Where the pastor is blocked, defensive, arrogant, anxious, compulsive, power-seeking or otherwise flawed his or her leadership will be distorted by these needs. Where needs remain denied or are unacknowledged this distortion will be hidden. It may lead to a replacement of group facilitation by the pastor's need to use the group for his or her own inner purposes. For example, if as a pastor I am anxious on account of my own tendency to agnosticism, a fear I do not like to admit to myself, it may interfere with my ability to encourage members of the church group to face up to their own doubts. Or if I easily feel insecure when a group member shows qualities of leadership it may inappropriately lead me to do all I can to maintain the group's dependence on me as their leader. Conversely if I have an exaggerated need for acceptance I may duck my responsibility to exercise any control of the group, with chaotic consequences.

A group leader therefore needs a certain self-knowledge. If the distortion described above is too great the pastor ineluctably falls into the leadership traps unearthed in Bion's discoveries about basic assumptions. Where leaders are vulnerable through their own need, they will collude with the group's idealization of them as magic leaders upon whom the group may be all-dependent. Or they may find themselves leading the fight against a common enemy, even creating one, which their rational self if they could only tune into it would know to be wild, paranoid fantasy.

Sufficient self-knowledge, then, is needed by the pastor to enable the irrational fantasies of the group to be dispelled by the non-collusion of the leader. And it is needed so that pastors may exercise self-control in their response when something occurs in the group to provoke an automatic reaction in them. Clearly my self knowledge is not the same as my ability to manipulate my own inner world. The most perspicacious person is still a constant victim of their own compulsorily triggered internal reactions. But if such reactions are recognized and acknowledged they can be sufficiently taken account of so as not to interfere with the leadership task of enabling the group. For example, if I recognize that the merest hint of male chauvinism instantly ignites my anger and I sense that the male chauvinism of some group members is a problem, I can assist the group to tackle this better if I put brackets round my own inner anger and remain free to lead the group as a whole.

(b) *Generalist pastoral skills*
The point here is the obvious but essential one that every pastoral skill possessed by the leader will be a necessary asset in his or her leadership: listening, gentleness, empathy, genuine caring, courage, willingness not to avoid pain or conflict—any pastoral quality comes into its own in the leadership of a small group.

(c) *Accepting the responsibilities of leadership*
A group leader is the focus of expectations and authority in the group. The group has a right to expect the leader to offer an initial structure, to maintain safe boundaries and to be sufficiently directive to ensure that the group begins to develop. Leaders must be clear that the leadership role does not allow them to be ordinary members of the group. They may wish to participate in the group even to the extent of sharing their own feelings or commenting on their own needs, but their eyes will never waver from the leadership task. For example, an ordinary group member may find himself expressing his difficulty with another member of the group. It is hardly appropriate for the leader to respond on the same level as another ordinary group member with his or her own feelings about this conflict. The leader's task is rather to 'manage the boundary'. This might mean ensuring that the conflict is worked through without turning into a fight; or recalling the group to its agreed task instead of becoming a row between two people; or simply ensuring that the group meeting finishes at the agreed time. Groups are not served by the leadership vacuum which would ensue from the

designated leader's attempt to be an ordinary member of the group. Leaders must meet their own needs of group membership elsewhere.

Groups need a leader to manage the boundaries so that individual members can feel free to explore what lies within them. Members need to feel safe. They need to feel that what goes on in the group will keep within agreed limits and that someone in the group will ensure this safety. If the designated leader is not willing to provide this fundamental lead, the group energy is spent on worrying about who will lead instead. The crucial distinction is between leadership which enables the group to develop and work through its stages of growth, and leadership which attempts to stifle the group: between power which is used to serve the group and power to which the leader clings.

(d) *Understanding how groups work*

Within the basic knowledge of group processes described above a pastor needs the skill to read what is going on in the group. Once the basic dynamics have been grasped variations on the fundamental theme need to be heard. Let us put the people we know from St Luke's, Stressville into a Bible Study group with their Vicar, Gerald Perkins, and observe what happens.

Clauda, Stephen and Joy always have strong ideas about what the Bible passage means. It is as if they are trying to take charge of the meeting. But Stephen and Joy are constantly arguing. Trev and Henry feel permanently angry during meetings. They resent the way Stephen, Clauda and Joy control them. Trev in particular has suggested various ideas about the Bible passage which he felt were rejected outright by Stephen. Trev and Henry are starting to say they are no longer learning anything, that the group is a waste of time. Henry has said, 'the Bible is supposed to build up love—all this group does is argue and destroy it. Whenever I say anything I'm treated as really stupid'. Henry soon intends to leave. Ruth and Charlie and Lillian hardly ever say anything. Charlie is bored. Lillian is frustrated. Ruth is torn between her admiration of Stephen's Bible knowledge and support for Henry when Stephen undermines Henry's attempts to contribute. She is fearful of what others think of her. She keeps her thoughts and feelings to herself. The pastor does not need complex technical theories to understand the gist of what is happening in this group. He or she can *read* it from what is being said, how things are said, who says them, and what is *not* said. The group has developed factions. Clauda, Stephen and Joy have come to be seen as powerful, if not bossy. Perhaps they arouse Trev's and Henry's envy. Clearly there is rivalry between Joy and Stephen. Trev and Henry appear to feel 'got at' by the 'bossy' faction, which they resent. Trev feels his ideas have been trampled on. Henry feels excluded, a pain which he feels no one else notices. Ruth, Charlie, Lillian are caught in between. They are reluctant to ally with one of the other two factions for fear of being rejected by the other. So both their hostility and creativity remain unspoken. Inevitably, the morale of the group is very low. The Bible passages, which so interested the group in the first few meetings, now seem boring, as if they have little to offer. But it is not the Bible which has changed. The group has got stuck and is likely to remain so, or suffer a further loss of morale, until Gerald Perkins, the vicar can help them to see what has happened and see how they are viewing one another through a distorting screen rather than as they actually are.

Groups will generally carry a balance of feelings. All human beings are able to experience a range of feelings, some pleasant others very unpleasant. Even within the course of one day, it is common for a person's feelings to include the swing from happy to sad, enthusiastic to depressed and angry to peaceful. When a *group* of people come together it would be surprising if this variety of feelings were not in *some* way present. The pastor's task is to help keep the balance. For example, if the group appears to contain nothing but positive feelings—the group is beautiful, life is beautiful, even the leader is beautiful—the pastor might begin to wonder where the opposition, anger, or rivalry have gone to. And vice versa. In the example from St Luke's the necessary pastoral task would be to restore a more realistic balance of feelings. Had the various factions stopped listening to each other? Were they not being perceived in a very distorted way? Did the 'bossy' members really not want to respond to the creativity in the rest of the group? Could not the 'got at' group express their anger constructively and once again contribute in a more fulfilling way? The leader's task is to enable the group as far as possible to *stay in reality* rather than become lost in exaggeration, fantasy, false expectations, failure to listen, distorted vision, one-sidedness and lack of balance.

Whether the *content* of the group is a Bible Study, a PCC, a Lent Group, or whatever it is, the pastor must keep an eye on the *process* as well, and be prepared to intervene gently at that level. However enthusiastic Gerald Perkins is about the parables of Luke (or whatever the group is discussing) he fails as a pastor if he is not aware of, say, Henry's sense of exclusion or Ruth's hesitancy and so fails to offer the appropriate encouragement, or, for example, to check the domination of the group by Stephen or Clauda: 'We've heard quite a lot about Stephen and Clauda's reaction to the parable and I was wondering whether those who haven't said anything yet might like to share their thoughts', might be a sufficient lead to enable Henry or Ruth to contribute again to the group.

(e) *Keeping the group on target*
Groups have been distinguished by social scientists as *task groups* organized for a particular job and *sentient* (or *primary* or *church family*) *groups* that require and receive loyalty from their members. The distinction can be illustrated in a diagram:

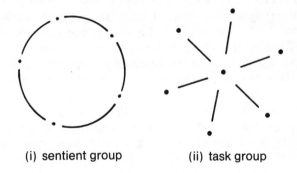

(i) sentient group   (ii) task group

In (i) the loyalty and attachment is invested in the relations between group members; in (ii) the individual members are joined to the task at the centre.

The pastor's role is to assist the group to stay on its particular target. Most often this is by:

— explicit reminders as to the task;
— helping the group to work through inter-personal difficulties and necessary phases of growth so that it can make its energy available for the task realistically;
— providing authority and structure by such means as judicious use of the chair, organization of the agenda, intervening when irrelevant items are brought forward and firm management of the meeting.

In some groups loyalty to sentience must take precedence over loyalty to a practical task. For example, suppose you are the leader of a group of alcoholics whose need is for mutual support to the end of avoiding alcohol. And suppose I arrive and say, 'It's all right everyone, I've found a way we can all enjoy one drink a day.' Then the pastor clearly should *not* let that sentient group, whose aim is support, become a task group working to test out the validity of my new theory.

The PCC's task, however, is to work through its agenda. The pastor should clearly not allow it to proceed as if it were a support group instead. Let us suppose that discussion of music in church is known to upset Fred on the PCC. Nevertheless it cannot be right to switch the task from that of a music review to that of assisting Fred with his difficulties about music.

The pastor thus needs to be supple and flexible in guiding the group (again and again if need be) along the path of its purpose. He or she needs to be able to see what is causing any difficulty in staying on track, since it is not usually the case that the purpose is inadvertently 'forgotten'. Groups get stuck for a reason. Perhaps someone has withdrawn because they feel something they have not been able to voice: the pastor can help them to say it. Perhaps there is a hidden hostility or rivalry in the group: the pastor can help the group to face it. It is helpful for the pastor to remember that any fantasy the group members may have (e.g. if the anger in the group were admitted it would be devastating) this *is* nonetheless fantasy. The reality of (gently) letting the truth be heard is, in general, more liberating than its suppression. The same holds when for some reason the group has become demoralized. Group members may feel paralyzed as a result. The very thought of revitalization might seem madness. In fact it is the other way round. The demoralization, though doubtless understandable, can turn out, on examination, to have been a temporary captivity to feelings which, later, group members can hardly imagine ever having felt. In other words pastors need to trust that groups are not fixed, static entities, like statues round a Greek pantheon. The process *will* move on, given the appropriate facilitation.

However well prepared the pastor is, he or she will still have to experience the pain of destructive and hostile feelings. Occasionally a particular group will break down in apparent disarray. But the pastor should by no means write off what has happened: it still remains to be seen what phoenix rises from the ashes. I have known it take even years before members of a group which had seemed to go wrong discovered they had become friends. So while the breakers of group dynamics rise and fall, occasionally in a crash, the process of pastoral care must go steadily on. Pastoral care of a group is always provisional. Its aim is to assist the group into their future. Its focus of concentration is on the present, but it makes intelligent use of the story so far. A pastor must never succumb to the temptation of believing that *anything* is permanently fixed in the business of human relationships. Human feelings may get temporarily stuck like a block in a drain, but they don't get cemented in like bricks.

Notes

1. See, for example, D. S. Whitaker, *Using Groups to Help People,* Routledge and Kegan Paul 1985; P. B. Smith, *Group Processes and Personal Change,* New York, Harper and Row 1980; S. Thompson and J. H. Kahn, *The Group Process as a Helping Technique,* Pergamon 1970; or the classics: W. R. Bion, *Experiences in Groups,* Tavistock 1968; the A. K. Rice Institute Series, *Group Relations Reader 1,* and *Group Relations Reader 2,* Washington 1975, 1985.
2. R. A. Lambourne, 'Personal Reformation and Political Formation in Pastoral Care (Extracts)' in *Explorations in Health and Salvation,* University of Birmingham 1985, p. 186.
3. These titles are first found in B. W. Tuckman, 'Developmental sequences in small groups', *Psychological Bulletin* 63 1965, p. 384 but have been much taken up in the literature; see C. Handy, *Understanding Organizations,* Penguin 1986, p. 171.

ELEVEN

On Political Involvement

Blessed are they which do hunger and thirst after righteousness: for they shall be filled.

Matt. 5.6

1. Inescapable Involvement

Inner city churches are inescapably involved with politics. The disturbed man who wanders up the aisle shouting abuse during a Sunday service raises the question of mental health care and the policy of psychiatric hospital closure. The stream of homeless people who call at the church centre for food raise the question of housing responsibility. A scuffle between youth and police in the churchyard raises the question of order and law. The 30% of church members without jobs raises the question of employment. Ubiquitous poverty and multiple deprivation raise every fundamental question of social and economic policy in national politics. In theory a church can, with an effort, keep its hands unsullied. It is possible to go on constructing PCC agendas around which hymn book to use or whether the choirboys need new cassocks. But these discussions look pretty silly when they are drowned by the sound of the riot squad's sirens and illuminated by burning houses down the street.

Inner city churches inhabit the world of major political issues. In Parsnip-in-the-Wold one social policy may look very like another with neither making much difference. In a UPA an adjustment in one small area of policy, say police methods, can trigger a riot. Their location alone impels inner city congregations to make political choices. Protagonists on every side of an issue make their voices loudly heard. Many people are politically articulate and alert. The plea of innocence, of being unaware of the issue, is more obviously

162

unconvincing. *Not* to support X or join Y feels more like a *decision* than a letting alone from blissful ignorance. There is no escaping the political heat however isolationist you might have preferred to be. One way or another you are called upon to respond. To choose not to is, in the inner city, a highly political choice. The inevitability of political involvement requires us then to ask both *how* a church might be politically involved—what might constitute *appropriate* involvement—and how can a church's involvement be *effective*. These questions are this chapter's concern.

2.   Effective Involvement

Here is a brief summary of the sort of political issue a congregation might have to face.

In an inner city parish a general hospital has recently closed. The nearest hospital is now in the next borough. The journey means two buses and a twenty-minute walk, which can take anything up to an hour and a half. In emergencies ambulances now seem to take much longer to come, although the health authority dispute this. What is more, the health visitors' clinic has been moved from a central position in the neighbourhood to the back of a large and otherwise deserted block of disused Council offices. There is a general uproar about the move. In addition, permission has just been refused for this part of the borough to have a health centre. The western, more wealthy part of the borough has, on the other hand, been allocated a large sum of money for the provision of just such a centre. This grant was the result of a five-year community campaign by the (mostly middle-class) residents of that area. Also, a recent survey of local GPs has revealed that 45% of surgeries are using temporary doctors, 43% of the panel doctors are over sixty years old and none speaks Greek, despite a large Greek community in the area. The report described collaboration between doctors and other agencies as 'virtually non-existent and a disgrace'. The upshot of all this has been the formation of a so-called 'Health Emergency Campaign' by a loose association of local residents. They are extremely keen to enlist the support of the parish church.

You need to know that the congregation contains a member

of the area health authority, several nursing auxiliaries from the hospital, a health visitor, a doctor, three cleaners also employed at the hospital and a majority of people who feel angry about local health provision but whose political response varies widely.

The request for the church to support the 'Emergency Campaign' comes from a member of the PCC who is also active on the tenants' association most responsible for setting it up. He wants to put his request on the PCC agenda. The aims of the campaign are:

— To have a petition signed by as many people as possible, agencies and institutions to call upon the Health Authority to act immediately to
  (a) provide transport to the hospital
  (b) move the health visitors back to their old site
  (c) produce a proposal for the improved organization of general practice within five years.
— In three months' time to march to the Area Health Authority with this petition.

This is what happened at Church A:

The health authority member, when he heard, was outraged. He went straight round to the Vicar to say any association between the church and this campaign would be monstrous. These people had no idea of the harsh economic realities and the pressures under which the health authority acted. He didn't come to church to be personally attacked. He was furious at the idea that his professional work should be publicly debated by people who didn't know the half of it. He was sick and tired of attempts to turn the church into an adjunct of the Labour Party. The Vicar scented division and disaster. He telephoned Tom (the campaigner) and said this one was 'too hot to handle'. Individuals obviously could join the campaign, and he would consider joining himself. But clearly it couldn't be a matter for the PCC; it would lead to far more upset than good. What difference would it really make anyway even if they *did* join as a church? Surely not much. He hoped Tom wouldn't mind. He was so sorry. He did, personally, admire Tom's commitment enormously.

This is what happened at Church B:

The health authority member, when he heard, was outraged. He went straight round to the Vicar and made the same speech. The Vicar replied most sympathetically. Of course Arnold (the health authority member) was *bound* to be distressed by matters so close to himself being debated in church. It was most uncomfortable for him. He urged Arnold to see that for many parishioners this was also a tremendously sore issue. If they were ignorant of half the facts surely here was an opportunity to help them come to terms with the 'harsh realities'. What could be wrong with an honest discussion about the whole matter? Arnold must not take it personally. The important thing was to let everyone have their say and, as far as possible, help them to see what was realistic. But nothing could be achieved by keeping a tight lid on discussion. That would only make people boil the more. He suggested, as he showed Arnold to the door, that Arnold be invited to the next PCC, when it would surely be right to discuss this issue, but also right to let Arnold participate in the discussion if he wanted to do so.

For two weeks the parish hummed with discussion. At the PCC meeting, there was heated argument. Arnold did not come. The decision was to support individual church members in joining the campaign if they so wished, but not to join as a church. This was unanimous. Arnold was not too unhappy with this decision. Church life continued as normal.

This is what happened at Church C:

Arnold, when he heard, was outraged. His instinct was to go straight round to the Vicar. But he didn't. For one thing the Vicar was always out. More important, he remembered what happened the *last* time he went round to the Vicar in a stew. He got shown into the study and treated to sixty minutes blasted pastoral counselling or whatever they call it. Couldn't stand that again. He'd telephone Muriel, the church warden. She'd see sense. But he'd forgotten Muriel was a health visitor, and had already joined the campaign. 'I can guess why you've rung', Muriel began, 'but don't expect me to go with you on this one. I've always liked you, Arnold—this isn't something about you—but you've got to understand the position. You're a brave man coming to the church in your own health area and I admire you for it. But people are very upset around here. The best thing you can do till this whole thing is over, is to lie low. Either that or come in, face the music, and defend your own corner. Sorry Arnold, the church has got to take a stand here in the name of what's right, and I for one shall be voting to join in.'

In this church also the item got onto the agenda, but not without preparation. The week before, an evening was set aside for an 'Open Forum on Health Care in the Parish'. To start the discussion the doctor, Muriel, Arnold (who declined), a nursing auxiliary, a cleaner at the hospital and a parishioner whose husband had been in hospital for a month, were invited to comment on local provision for health as they saw it. 160 people attended including some from other churches or no church at all. There was a strong sense at the meeting that:

(a) the grievances of local people about health provision really were justified;

(b) the campaign had modest, realistic goals and should be supported.

At the PCC there was a heated discussion. The church decided to affiliate with the campaign by a majority of twelve to three. Muriel was reluctant to face Arnold on the following Sunday. She found herself hoping he wouldn't come, but loyalty goes deep with Arnold and he did. Thinking about it, Muriel realized that she was afraid of Arnold's anger. She was perceptive enough to see that the glee, at Arnold's expense, of those on the winning side might alienate him altogether from the church. Accordingly, and with some skill, she overcame her reluctance to speak to him and took Arnold on one side after the service. She reminded him of her respect for him and said: 'It's good for those of us who wanted to join, but you must still be feeling angry, Arnold.' He was, and Muriel enabled him to say so. Apart from his anger Arnold felt sure the health authority's case had not been properly argued. Muriel suggested he wrote a piece on this for the parish magazine. Rather to his own surprise, Arnold found himself agreeing.

R. H. Tawney defined politics as: 'The art of achieving by

collective action ends which cannot be attained with the same
measure of success by individuals acting in isolation.'[1]
Whether or not you support Church C's decision, and
irrespective of the subsequent success of the campaign,
Church C has acted politically and lived. It has faced up to
the issue as a church, attempted to examine the facts, made
judgements on the basis of what seemed needed and right,
and not been afraid to *act* on its conclusions. It has shown it
is possible to do more than follow the course which so many
churches believe is the only one available, to nail your colours
firmly to the fence. I do not say Church C was right in its
decision. I do say it was right in its willingness to consider
supporting a campaign whose aims it found more in alignment
with God's Kingdom than the political status quo. No one can
prescribe a programme of political involvement for a church.
But it can be both appropriate and effective, enhancing rather
than threatening parish life.

3. Appropriate Involvement

The task of seeking its political integrity is a very difficult one
for a church. The Church worldwide currently presents a
variety of models and examples of political involvement. How
is a local inner city church to find its political identity within
this? What theology might guide its political involvement
when there plainly exists such a wide divergence of opinions?
And even if it proved possible to make headway in theory, is
not the practice of political involvement such a pastoral
glacier that it would be better to cancel the trip than risk the
dangers of the crossing?

(a) *The influence of Liberation Theology and William Temple*

Some kind of political theology of liberation was bound to be
developed during this century. Sooner or later theologians
had to digest the significance of Marx's analysis and draw
upon it in their own writing. The Second Vatican Council can
be seen, at one level, as a sustained justification of
Christianity against the Marxist charge that 'because
Christians assert the existence of a coming Kingdom in which

compensating justice and mercy will be done, they can neglect the claims of this world.'[2] As the Council documents bluntly put it:

> If the demands of justice and equity are to be satisfied, vigorous efforts must be made . . . to remove as quickly as possible the immense economic inequalities which now exist.[3]

Of the far-reaching developments that have since taken place in the Roman Catholic Church, the most relevant to the inner city church is the Liberation Theology emerging from the Third World, especially that of Latin America. In Europe until recently, theology remained caught in the struggle to combat secularization and unbelief. When I was at University in the seventies the great thing for students of theology was to tease out the advantages of faith over atheism for personal fulfilment. No wonder such theology seemed beside the point when I got to the Elephant and Castle. Liberation Theology, on the other hand, seeks to discover how faith might be meaningful among the poor and marginalized, those rejected by society. The Liberation Theologians' question is exactly the one which struck me so forcibly as a curate, and which inner city churches have constantly to face: how is it possible to speak of God in a dehumanized world? Liberation Theology finally knocks on the head any idea that a divine purpose is so assuredly evolving in human history that the present injustice of social institutions can be tolerated. Liberation Theology revives the tradition of *prophecy* in which injustice is condemned right away and the call is made for a new political order based on the Christian vision.

As Liberation Theology has evolved so has its social analysis, its use of biblical and traditional theological material, its spirituality and its critique of western theology. But for our purpose its most significant development is not only the concept but the reality of basic communities. A leading Brazilian theologian, Leonardo Boff, introduces these in the following way:

> Modern society has produced a wild atomization of existence and a general anonymity of persons lost in the cogs. . . . There has been a reaction. Slowly, but with ever

increasing intensity, we have witnessed the creation of communities in which persons actually know and recognize each other, where they can be themselves . . . , where they can 'have their say', where they can be welcomed by name. And so, we see, groups and little communities have sprung up everywhere. This phenomenon exists in the church, as well: grassroots Christian communities, as they are known, or basic church communities.[4]

He continues:

Ever since the Medellin Conference (1968) this new ecclesial reality has been winning its citizenship, and today it constitutes, without a doubt, one of the great principles of church renewal worldwide . . . The communities are built on a more vital, lively, intimate participation . . . as their members seek to live the essence of the Christian message: the universal parenthood of God, communion with all human beings, the following of Jesus Christ who died and rose again, the celebration of the resurrection and the Eucharist, and the upbuilding of the Kingdom of God. . . . Christian life in the basic communities is characterized by the absence of alienating structures, by direct relationships, by reciprocity, by a deep communion, by mutual assistance, by communality of gospel ideals, by equality among members.[5]

The features shared by a Brazilian basic community and a renewed British inner city parish are clear: Boff's description could be of either. But British churches have not generally gone as far as Brazilian basic communities in the matter of politics. At the Fourth Inter-Church Meeting of Brazilian Basic Communities held in São Paulo in 1981, for example, the theme taken was 'The Church, an Oppressed People Organizing for Liberation'. One of their conclusions was that 'the capitalist system must be attacked in its roots'. Leonardo Boff was in São Paulo as a theological assessor. Of this conclusion he writes:

When it comes to identifying the causes of the miseries they suffer the members of the basic communities see the main one—not the only one, but the main one—as the capitalist system. But worse than the system itself is its individualistic spirit of accumulation, its social irresponsibility, and its insensitivity toward human beings, who are treated as 'man power' to be sold at auction. The communities denounce this as unjust, as contrary to God's design in history.[6]

The communities, in order to be politically effective, consider it necessary to work in unity with popular movements such as unions and neighbourhood associations. 'Politics', as the Conference's final letter stated, 'is the mighty weapon we have to build a just society the way God wants it.' The basic communities see their raised political consciousness as flowing from their religion. As Boff puts it, their political commitment is not 'the fruit of some leftist ideological infiltration but of reading the handbook of faith, the Bible, and of an attempt to understand it in the context in which it was written,' that is 'in communities of poor people, nearly always under the domination of foreign powers and yearning for integral liberation.'[7]

Faith in the City pays tribute to Liberation Theology as a possible inspiration for an indigenous UPA theology: 'Such a theology', it says, 'would start . . . from the personal experience, the modes of perception and the daily concerns of local people themselves.'[8] This is important, but why not an indigenous politics? Already Liberation Theology has been sufficiently absorbed into Roman Catholic teaching to have found official expression in the phrase 'the preferential option for the poor'. UPA churches, in collaboration with other community agencies, have a responsibility to work out what the political realities of such a 'preferential option' might look like. For example, the large, faceless bureaucracies of the borough town halls might be replaced by local offices at which people could be known by name. This might offset the great frustration now experienced in attempting to ask for a repair, query the rent or make a complaint about noise. But such a change requires a grass roots movement to inspire it.

Inner city churches are well placed to contribute to such an indigenous politics because, if they are doing their job, they will be impressively aware of local human needs. And they will already be in collaboration with community work going on in the parish. The point will be quickly made that the social and political context out of which Liberation Theology has been born is very different from the British situation. This is true, but it does not detract from the opportunity churches here have of learning from the *ecclesiogenesis* of Latin America. ? hllr!

Imported political theologies are not the only source of political inventiveness available to British churches. We have our own tradition, one which gave thought to the issue of the Church and politics in the modern world decades before the Second Vatican Council. This tradition finds best expression in the writing of Archbishop William Temple. His description of the relation between the Church and politics has in some respects not been surpassed. This passage from *Christianity and Social Order* is particularly apt:

> The method of the Church's impact upon society at large should be twofold. The Church must announce Christian principles and point out where the existing social order at any time is in conflict with them. It must then pass on to Christian citizens, acting in their civic capacity the task of re-shaping the existing order in closer conformity to the principles. For at this point technical knowledge may be required and judgements of practical expediency are always required. If a bridge is to be built, the Church may remind the engineer that it is his obligation to provide a really safe bridge: but it is not entitled to tell him whether, in fact, his design meets this requirement: a particular theologian may also be a competent engineer, and, if he is, his judgement on this point is entitled to attention: but this is altogether because he is a competent engineer and his theological equipment has nothing whatever to do with it. In just the same way, the Church may tell the politician what ends the social order should promote; but it must leave to the politician the devising of the precise means to those ends.

This is a point of first-rate importance, and is frequently misunderstood. If Christianity is true at all it is a truth of universal application; all things should be done in the Christian spirit and in accordance with Christian principles. 'Then', say some, 'produce your Christian solution of unemployment.' But there neither is nor could be such a thing. Christian faith does not by itself enable its adherent to foresee how a vast multitude of people, each one partly selfish and partly generous, and an intricate economic mechanism, will in fact be affected by a particular economic or political innovation — 'social credit', for example. 'In that case', says the reformer — or, quite equally, the upholder of the status quo — 'keep off the turf. By your own confession you are out of place here'. But this time the Church must say 'No; I cannot tell you what is the remedy; but I can tell you that a society of which unemployment (in peace time) is a chronic feature is a diseased society, and that if you are not doing all you can to find and administer the remedy, you are guilty before God'. Sometimes the Church can go further than this and point to features in the social structure itself which are bound to be sources of social evil because they contradict the principles of the Gospel.[9]

What can inner city churches take from this? It reminds them that their first task is to discern what the Christian principles are and where their local social situation is in conflict with them. This in itself is a formidable task of analysis. The church is not 'entitled' to devise political policy from Christian principle, but this does not justify political sloth by the Church with regard to policy. The first point is a proper reminder as to the limits of theology. The second would be irresponsible failure to use God-given intelligence. It seems clear that if some policies spell social disaster (such as, I would argue, massive cuts in social services or reduction of the rate support grant) a local church might rightly object. If other policies seemed exactly designed to enhance community well-being (for instance, an increase in the number of primary school teachers) the local church would be right to applaud. Nevertheless Temple's warning is important. In a complex socio-economic system detailed policies cannot be derived from Christian principles. Members of the congregation will disagree profoundly on matters of political policy, considering their own preference does *greater* justice to the Christian precept they think is involved. This alone would make political involvement a thorny pastoral issue. But it is more complex than simply a matter of how rational disagreements are resolved.

(b) *The pastoral tightrope*

Though inner city churches are continually confronted by political issues, it does not follow that their congregations are full of politically active people. On the contrary many inner city residents are passive about politics. They may have strong feelings or grievances and be quite willing, at home or in the pub, to argue vociferously with the politician on TV; they may go for a drink at the Liberal Club, proclaim themselves a diehard Conservative, Union man or Socialist but never think of themselves as having a political role beyond their right to vote in elections. Politics is very widely conceived of as something done by 'them' over against which one is powerless. Of course the context here is a society in which the possession of personal liberties is proudly boasted of, and a basis of well-being for all considered assured. The notorious conservatism (small c) of the traditional British working class must be understood against the background of the freedom and social stability they take for granted. On the other hand inner cities also contain large numbers of perhaps the *most* politically active groups anywhere to be found. Those who, for whatever reason, have been jolted out of their passivity can begin to see that *none* of the intransigent problems around them, such as bad housing or poor health care provision, will be remedied without forceful political lobbying. This is not always a division between educated idealists (nearly all left-wing) plus disaffected, angry young people, and traditional working class men and women in full employment. Many inner city political campaigns are *local* and *specific* rather than general and ideological. They arise from the need to save a hospital, school or bus service, or to renovate a decaying estate. These are the lobbies which more successfully mobilize local solidarity in a given neighbourhood. In general though, the politically passive live cheek by jowl with the politically most committed. If a church congregation represents its community it is therefore likely to contain people in both camps. The first pastoral question is how these opposites can be reconciled.

Let us imagine a situation in which 70% of the congregation believe that 'the church should stay out of politics' but 30% believe the opposite: that the church has an important role in helping bring about political change. What to do?

Inevitably this is a pastoral minefield reminiscent of the motorbike test in which bollards placed at awkward intervals must be avoided. Let us take the line followed by the Second Vatican Council, Liberation Theology, William Temple, and *Faith in the City* and agree, at least broadly, with the 30%. Can they achieve their aim only by offending and alienating the 70%? The answer, in my experience, is 'No'. But they will need to be patient. If your faith is not one in which politics connects with the Christian vision it will take time for you to learn that it might. If learning is to take place it must be mutual. Views on both sides must be listened to, understood and *respected*. The views of the 30% will need to be expressed in relation to those of the majority. They must be recast taking (as a starting point) the view of those who differ. Frequent reference must be made to those other views and their truth and value emphasized. The 30% need to share frankly the limitations and dangers of their own views. The aim is not to set up a confrontation and win it. It is to establish an atmosphere of dialogue in which it is acceptable for differences to exist with respect on both sides. This requires resilience, tact, openness and a certain assurance. Above all it demands the recognition of the emotional vulnerability which for so many people surrounds political issues. Arguments are very rarely just about their explicit and rational content. The man who storms out of church because 'South Africa' is mentioned in the intercessions turns out to have a cluster of very painful feelings into which the mention of 'South Africa' was a door. The feminist woman who refuses to talk to anyone who won't sign her petition turns out to be sitting on feelings of deepest anger of which she is not yet aware. For the man who weeps when the Vicar invites local politicians to debate in church, this invitation tramples on a lifetime of religious sensibility. The people who lobby against letting the church hall be used by a black community group are fuelled in their prejudice by years of reinforcement from family and peers. All these inner scenarios need to be appreciated. Human beings will not be knocked into a change of heart, however enlightened the advocates of reform may consider themselves, or however urgent the cause.

Even if an atmosphere of dialogue is established and it

becomes possible (in general) to discuss issues of politics as a normal aspect of church life, there still remains the difficult question of what kind of political intervention is appropriate for a local church. The problem, briefly put, is this. If the church throws in its lot with a specific political cause, such as the Movement for the Ordination of Women or the Campaign Against the Arms Trade, it is in danger of alienating those who, in conscience, oppose this cause. But if a church refuses thus to throw in its lot it is in effect siding with the *status quo*. This is the nub of the difficulty. Acquiescence with the *status quo* is the same as supporting it. This dilemma is unavoidable and fundamental. Its presence means that no deeper principle can make it right for a church *always* to choose one solution rather than the other. Rather it will always be necessary to consider issues on their own merits and make separate judgements in individual cases. In the present climate popular analysis is all too willing to label individuals and institutions as 'left-wing', 'fascist', 'trendy liberal' or 'Thatcherite'. Clearly a church must try to avoid making the package of predictable affiliations which inevitably set them up for such a label. It does not serve the church, for example, if the minister can be written off by his opponents as a 'trendy leftie'. All periods produce stereotyped labels of abuse such as 'Lollard', 'papist', 'Whig' and 'Bolshevik'. Their appearance signals that one side has stopped listening to the other.

It is easy to fall into the trap of onesidedness. If you feel powerless and angry maybe only the more successful protest organizations and opposition parties offer you any hope of radical change. In the circumstances of a 'right-wing' government this means it is tempting to want to be, and to be seen to be 'left-wing'. You wear all the right badges to display the point. Equally, piqued by the constant opposition and hostility, it is not surprising if those on the 'right' similarly make themselves visible. This identification swiftly becomes too obvious. What to you is a strong expression of your hope is written off by others as the predictable prejudice of a certain type of person. What is intended by you as a challenge becomes for others a signal not to take you seriously.

In the inner city this has to some extent happened between young people and the police, between those who support recent educational change and those who do not, between those who approve of the government and those who oppose it, between feminists and non-feminists and between those on different sides in the nuclear arms debate. Churches have a primary political responsibility to resist such polarization. They must avoid association with this dialogue of the deaf. On the contrary, their role is to translate slogans and clichés back into the vivid and specific language needed to describe the human situation as it is, parish problems as they are and injustice as they see it. And their pastoral responsibility is to assist genuine dialogue to start again.

Notes

1. R. H. Tawney, *The Radical Tradition*, Allen and Unwin 1964, p. 89.
2. P. Hebblethwaite, *The Runaway Church*, Collins 1975, p. 181.
3. Pastoral Constitution on the Church in the Modern World (*Gaudium et Spes*), in A. Flannery, ed., *Vatican Council II: Conciliar and Post-Conciliar Documents*, Dublin, Dominican Publications 1981.
4. L. Boff, *Ecclesiogenesis*, Collins 1986, p. 1.
5. ibid., p. 4.
6. ibid., p. 42.
7. ibid., p. 41.
8. *Faith in the City*, p. 65.
9. W. Temple, *Christianity and Social Order*, SPCK 1976, pp. 58-59. For more recent contributions from a Church of England bishop to this debate see D. E. Jenkins, *God, Politics and the Future*, SCM 1988.

TWELVE

A Pastoral Visiting Scheme for the Whole Congregation

And he said to them, 'The harvest is plentiful but the labourers are few.'

Luke 10.2

What would you do if your neighbour's husband were sent to prison for armed robbery, or her daughter fatally injured in a car crash? You might want to visit her, but be held back from doing so by lack of confidence. In a UPA parish, the need for pastoral visiting is great. In one year, a parish might be responsible for perhaps one hundred funerals, eighty baptisms and fifty marriages. At any one time there may be thirty or more parishioners in hospital. There is a constant flow of new residents into the parish. If the parish has a church school there are parents or prospective parents to visit. Altogether the church may have had some contact with perhaps two thousand people in about two years. Perhaps a family come to church sufficiently often to have filled in an address form. Maybe a family called at the Vicarage because they had run out of food. Perhaps someone in the family attempted suicide and the clergy were involved. Perhaps the church knows where the parish's elderly and isolated people live . . . and so on. Obviously, these figures need considerable adjustment from parish to parish. But the idea of a Pastoral Visiting Scheme for the whole congregation arose from the calculation that, according to parish statistics, I was about four thousand visits behind as a Vicar. This laughable situation engendered the thought that one hundred and fifty people at two visits a week could remedy the backlog in three months. A fantasy of course, and, in any case, the point of pastoral visiting is not to barge round the parish mopping up regrettable statistics. But a serious idea had taken root. If we could develop a modest training scheme to fit the purpose, why could not the majority of members of the congregation be assisted to play their part in parish pastoral care over the years ahead? Clearly some people have much more time to give than others. But we thought that a well devised training scheme would be something which most people would feel they could gain from and be willing to take on as a part of their church stewardship.

What follows does not claim to be a perfect scheme. It is an outline of one way of approaching the training of pastoral visitors and it has the merit of having been tried and tested in an inner city parish. It was devised jointly by Mrs Jan McGregor, a social worker trainer (and member of the congregation) and me in the summer of 1984 for the parish of Holy Trinity, Tottenham.

Setting up the Scheme

In order to devise the training sessions, we needed to answer these preliminary questions:

What commitment were we asking for?
How would the scheme be introduced to the church?
What would be the scope of the pastorate?
How would the scheme be operated and co-ordinated?
What follow-up to training and support would be needed?

We decided that it was important to emphasize from the start that in our understanding the *church* was the resource, not the pastoral visitors as autonomous individuals. Naturally the visitors would use their own gifts, but their visit would be as a church representative. We knew that volunteer schemes often foundered when volunteers became overwhelmed by the weight of someone else's burden on their own shoulders. We wanted to emphasize that it was the church as a whole who would contain the final responsibility, not the individual visitor. Visitors were to think of themselves as participating in the church's healing task. This would help to keep them free from an inappropriate sense of responsibility, a sense that they ought to be able to make problems disappear or painful emotional states vanish into thin air. We settled for a twofold commitment: to attend *all* the six training sessions (of one and a half hours each); and to make at least *one* visit between support groups (once a month). This minimum does not prevent those who can from making more visits. We decided to introduce the scheme to the church in four ways: a discussion in the PCC; an explanation of the proposals, with an accompanying sermon two months before the start; an article in the church magazine; and an exhibition at the back of church. We regarded the first course as a pilot scheme from which we could learn.

We said somewhat boldly that the training would be suitable both for those with no previous pastoral training or experience and for those who had already received training (such as counselling training), and for several reasons. First, there is always more to learn about oneself in relation to others and secondly, we assumed that the church orientation and implicit theology of the scheme would be new for most people. We also wanted to emphasize the corporate aspect of the care scheme as emanating from a fellowship—a team of visitors who would have a particular belonging together in training which would continue in the support group. However, our main aim was to enrol those in the congregation who wanted to be able to assist more formally in parish pastoral care but who so far lacked the confidence to do so. Our eventual aim was, as implied above, to provide an 'extensive' training for most people in the congregation, *not* to produce an initial twelve 'special' people. Confining it to an initial twelve was for purely practical reasons.

Since we felt that the potential scope of the pastorate was too large to be manageable we decided to limit it to the following groups:

1 New people who came to church;
2 Parents and prospective parents of the church school;
3 Families of those young people known at church;
4 Families known by having had children baptized at church;
5 Couples who had been married in church;
6 The bereaved;
7 Parishioners known to be lonely, handicapped or disturbed;

8 Those in trouble with the police;
9 Referrals from professional agencies (e.g. Social Services, doctors, Probation Office, clergy from beyond the parish).

You might think this scope to be daringly if not dangerously wide. But at least to define the limits meant the scheme was protected from a sense of feeling guilty for not immediately responding to every verbal request to have someone from the church visit Mrs Jones at no. 22 by teatime today. We had to face the fact that although everyone has a contribution to make to parish pastoral care, not everyone would be suitable for the training course. Our ambitions would inevitably be limited by the problem of some people's inappropriate personality. We considered the training would be suitable for people who could (given the necessary help) put others at their ease, give confidence, and make a provisional assessment of need and thus at least be a contact. We further thought potential visitors should be people who (again with help) could contain their own tendency to make judgements on others, accept help themselves and be 'Christ-bearing'.

We expected this to make most regular members of the congregation eligible for the scheme. As it happened all those who wanted to join the first training group were, in our view, sufficiently suitable. Our selection criteria were not the strict ones required perhaps by, say, a voluntary counselling service. For although some of the visiting we had in mind—such as to the depressed, the angry or the bereaved—could not even be considered unless visitors had achieved a recognizable degree of empathetic sensitivity and advanced pastoral skill, we also aimed to use the scheme in situations where the visitor's aim would be the more modest one of, for example, bringing a welcome from the church to a family whose child was about to enter the church's primary school. The scheme co-ordinator would have to try hard to match the responsibility of a visitor's task to his or her limitations. For example, the visitor might be restricted to visiting those known to need help with their shopping and to offer assistance in this way. Clearly this was not a foolproof guarantee that a visitor's approach or style would be appropriate, but it was an important control. We also put some faith in the assumption that inappropriate visitors would be weeded out by their failure to keep the ground rules of the training programme. Besides attendance at every session these included punctuality, confidentiality and, when visiting began, completion of the pro forma and attendance at the support group. We were prepared, if necessary, to refuse entry to the training scheme if we found ourselves unable to give someone the initial benefit of the doubt. As vicar I would have taken responsibility for this on the basis, obviously, of trying to help the person concerned, and discovering what contribution to parish life would be more suitable for them.

Outline of the Training Course Sessions

Session 1: Introduction and Boundaries

Each session lasts an hour and a half. Participants are briefed that all sessions will keep to time and are asked to be punctual themselves. A coffee (or tea) break of no more than five minutes takes place at about half-time. The break is important. It offers respite, a brief relaxation of tension, the opportunity to socialize as a whole group (however briefly—it still seems to be worth it) and a natural break when moving from one phase of the session to the next.

The input of Session 1 concerns *boundaries* and their significance. *Punctuality*, already mentioned, is one boundary. *Confidentiality* is another. Clearly it is essential to contract from the start that the group must respect the confidentiality of what is said either concerning a member of the group or someone outside it. Equally important are *personal boundaries*. People need to realize what they can take on, or share, or risk and when a personal boundary has been reached. And they need to learn not to cross the boundaries of others.

After the initial introduction there is an introductory exercise. The group is divided into twos. For ten minutes half the group introduce themselves to the other half describing themselves and their lives in any way that they wish. Then they swap over and the other half introduce *themselves*. The whole group then reassembles. At this point (and without prior warning) group members are asked to introduce their partner to the group on the basis of what has been said (but so as to respect confidentiality). Some people will have listened more attentively than others, who will be quick (and pained) to learn the point. This takes a further thirty minutes, and is followed by the break.

The final twenty-five minutes are given to eliciting the expectations of course members. In two groups of six people each set of expectations are 'brainstormed' and written onto large sheets of paper. When each group has completed the task they compare their summary charts to see where they have either concurred or differed. The purpose of 'brainstorming' expectations is threefold. It is a means by which everyone is able to state their hopes of the course as an individual; it enables the organizers to respond to what participants want, letting them feel that they 'own' the course rather than experiencing it as being dictated to them from on high; and it provides a means of evaluation at the end of the course. Participants can look back at their initial expectations, particularly their apprehensions and anxieties, and see (or feel) how far they have come. They can also see what the gaps are, what the course has *not* covered and what they feel is yet to be learned.

Session 2: Interviewing Techniques

The title makes this session sound perhaps clinical and impersonal. In fact its aim is the opposite: to begin to discover how a sensitively conducted interview can leave someone in need feeling better. As a pastoral visitor I need to discover my own style as an interviewer. Once I have experienced how it feels to share something myself I can start to see what enables someone to share a problem and what might block this process. The notion of 'process' has already been introduced in Chapter Ten above on the small group. It refers to everything going on in communication that can be distinguished from the transcribable content of what is actually said. Visitors will need to learn how the process and content belong together; if the process is being blocked (e.g. because as a visitor I signal boredom by my constant yawning) the content will also be blocked (e.g. the visited person may simply not tell me the story of how her husband died and the loneliness she has felt ever since). In the training course it is therefore important to model good group process. Hence the emphasis on punctuality and confidentiality.

Allied to these is a further issue concerning group process to which leaders will need to pay attention. If group members leave a session ruffled in some way, perhaps because someone else irritated them, or they felt left out or hurt, they will be strongly tempted afterwards to pour out their feelings to one or other member of the group, or to one of the leaders. The leaders themselves will therefore need to take care to confine their discussions of issues and feelings arising from the course to the sessions rather than let them be discussed from time to time throughout the week. It is, in any case, tempting for course members to want to make their own relationship with the leaders special in some way. It is reassuring to feel you stand out from the other group members. To ask questions or raise general or personal issues outside the course sessions is a way to achieve this special status. To assist the proper maintenance of boundaries here, there must be a space for discussing 'leftover feelings'. In this course it took the form of a short period at the start in which members of the group were invited to share any such feelings (whether positive, negative or ambivalent) left over from the previous week.

Outline Plan of Session 2.

Prayer (five minutes) which usefully reminds members that the task and its context are rooted in God.

Leftover Feelings (five minutes) The leader here has to keep to the approximate time boundary of five minutes (otherwise the prepared content of the session will be thrown into jeopardy) whilst at the same time enabling this short period to feel like an unhurried space which has room to take seriously what members wish to say. If this space for leftover feelings is cramped, the unvoiced hostility (or whatever feelings are bubbling away just below the surface) will be in danger of sabotaging the content of the session. Those who do not feel fully involved or who have a problem with the leadership may withdraw their co-operation (perhaps without even realizing they are doing so).

Part One (forty minutes—up to the break) The idea that some things are harder to share than others is introduced. A short space is given for people to think of something about themselves they would:

(a) readily share with anyone;
(b) only be willing to share with friends;
(c) not be willing to share with *anyone* (except perhaps one or two very close friends).

The group is then asked if someone would be willing to offer something *slightly* hard to share about themselves with the group in the course of an interview: not a devastating secret, just something they would mildly rather people in general did not know. When someone has bravely volunteered, a second volunteer is needed to be interviewer. It is a good idea for the leaders to remind the group that during the course everyone will be expected to volunteer for *something* (e.g. to take part in a role play) on a fairly equal basis. This tends to encourage a flow of volunteers from the start as some people always want to get such tribulations over with as soon as possible.

Attention must be paid to how the room is set out for the interview. An appropriate interviewing area must be distinguished from the part of the room where the observer will be; the interview chairs must be appropriately spaced, and so on. The observers also need to be told with some firmness how damaging it will be to the process of the interview if they do not keep still and quiet. Reaction, such as laughter, is not appropriate. In my experience, a leader may have to remind the group several times about this. It may even be necessary to interject a sharp 'shh'. It is natural for the group to react since what is going on is not without tension. But a clear briefing as to *why* reaction gets in the way should prevent it.

Then follows the interview in which one person assists the other to express their chosen 'slightly hard thing to share about themselves'. The interview will doubtless run for some minutes and the leader halts it at a suitable time. Discussion follows in which the leaders add their remarks and questions. They will also need to see how those who have taken part in the interview feel and, where necessary, facilitate any further resolution of feelings.

Break for tea or coffee (five minutes) There is no time to start boiling kettles at this juncture. The drinks must be produced immediately!

After the break (thirty minutes) There should now be time for a second interview along the same lines, but with two different people.

Conclusion It is a good idea to leave a few minutes at the end to ventilate feelings and reactions in general, and for prayer.

Session 3: Getting in touch with feelings

Session 3 makes use of role play which must be carefully introduced. The prospect of role play raises anxieties and, not infrequently, resistance. This is understandable. Role play arouses feelings, which have the power to make participants vulnerable. People feel, not surprisingly, that they will be giving something away by taking part in a role play. Therefore leaders must emphasize that role play is being used only because it is a creative means of training for a particular task, a tool to help you learn to do a task on behalf of the church. It is not a shift from learning, to, say, therapy.

Resistance to role play takes predictable forms. It will be said that it is 'artificial', 'not like real life' and 'contrived'. This is of course true in a sense. It *is* artificial in that the situations are fiction and entered into by those whose life circumstances are different. But it is *not* artificial in the sense that the feelings it draws on are real feelings; the situations are sufficiently familiar to the participants *in terms of their emotional landscape* to be invaluable in human relations training. The crucial point of training with role play is that it works. No amount of reading, lectures, seminars or group discussion can achieve the learning which can occur as the result of one good session using role play. It works as a means of entering the realm of feelings and reflecting upon their significance.

The use of role play needs skilful handling by the leader. The group may need to be wooed, just a little, for them to have the confidence to agree. Members of the group will need directive and clear but very simple guidance from the leaders as to exactly what is expected. At a certain point though, when character guidelines have been given, the leader must let the participants launch out on their own. Whatever the outcome of the role-play it may be important to 'de-role' the participants as otherwise they may take their role home with them. At the end of a role play Jan McGregor commonly used to ask people their real names and what they had had for breakfast!

The aim of Session 3 is to help the visitor get in touch with *how it feels to be needy*. It is easy to condemn the way others are judgemental, defensive, prejudiced, bitter or aggressive, but what does it feel like from their end? Suppose you actually feel locked in to your bitterness, aggression or whatever, as if in a trap? What might help set you free? To learn this pastoral visitors need to encounter something of their *own* judgemental nature and defensiveness. Session 3 is designed to provide a structure for reflecting upon this. The role play can be used twice with a different group of participants each time. All the briefing participants need is one or two dominant character- istics of the person to be taken on. For the following role play the pastoral visitor is told: You are going to visit the family of John and Mary Smith. Dean Smith (aged eleven) goes to the church School and the visiting scheme is systematically visiting families of the church School children who are not known in church. You also know that not long ago 'Nan' Smith (John's mother) lost her husband and that she now lives with the family. The family members are told:

John Smith: You are known as Dad. You are a bus driver in your late forties. You are authoritarian, chauvinistic and racist. You have no time for the church.

Mary Smith: You are known as Mum. You feel *very* bad about not going to church. You don't fight your husband but are compliant towards him.

Michelle Smith: You are sixteen and a half and unemployed. You have a black boyfriend called Glenroy. You are not speaking to your father at present on account of his attitude to Glenroy.

Nan: You lost your husband (Grandad) six months
              ago and have moved in with the rest of the
              family. You are still very upset. You are
              John's mother.

One evening you are all sitting round the TV when the
doorbell goes.

The role play may run for as long as fifteen minutes. Use can
be made of 'doubling' in which an observer temporarily takes
over a particular role by standing behind a particular
character and putting their hands on his or her shoulders.
The leader may intervene if appropriate, perhaps if the visitor
gets stuck. It can be very useful, at the end, to ask characters
to stay *in role* while the leader interviews them about 'how
they felt when . . .' or how they are left feeling.

Session 4: Different Personality Types

The title is not intended to imply that people can be neatly
packaged into types. Rather the potential visitor learns how
to discover why the visited person perhaps has such a
powerful effect on them (making them feel guilty, or angry for
example). Help in these circumstances can come when the
visitor is able to slough off the manipulation of that particular
personality type and respond to them 'intact'. It may be
possible to help the visited person see something of the effect
they have on others and be released from the self-paralysis of
their own behaviour. It will be important to the visitor to
discern such different personality types as the aggressive
person, the guilt-inducing person, the person who projects
their feelings or the rationalizing person, and to become
aware of what defences may be at work in sustaining them.
For example if, as a visitor, I visit an elderly lady living alone
and within the first ten minutes I have

  — promised to get the Vicar to visit as soon as possible;
  — offered to do the weekly shopping;
  — consented to find someone to mend a light fitting;
  — promised to come back next Tuesday and made a start
    on the washing;

I am probably not handling the demands of my old lady very
well! But it is not easy. She is firing volleys of demand at me,
complaining no one cares, buttering me up with her flattery
as to how I'm the kindest person she's ever met . . . it's easy to
succumb and say yes. At least until you manage to get
yourself out of the door . . . never to return. But that's the
story of this lady's life. That's *why* nobody goes round. A
church pastoral visitor needs to learn how to sidestep the
demands of the old lady without rejecting her as a person.
Indeed, as far as possible the visitor should introduce some
reality into the situation, assisting the old lady to learn what
she can and cannot have.

Session 4 thus makes use of two role plays, one before and
one after the break. The first is a visit to a depressed person,
who turns out to be sitting on a lot of unacknowledged anger.
In addition he or she is someone who is good at avoiding the
painful issues. The second role play is the classic one of the
guilt-inducing and demanding old lady as described above. It
may be important to find one of the group's more resilient
characters to volunteer that visit, preferably one with a sense
of humour!

Session 5: Bereavement

Session 5 is designed to help the pastoral visitor feel able to
make a visit to a bereaved person or family. Bereavement
visiting is a central feature of church-based pastoral care. To
say this is not in any way to devalue the marvellous area-
based secular bereavement projects which now exist, although
they are still rare. It is merely to note that one dimension of
facing up to death is a facing up to questions of ultimate
value and the possibility of some kind of hope for love beyond
the grave. This is a place where, particularly in our post-
christian society, living Christian faith can speak where little
or nothing else can. However, though the value of the scheme
may be evident in bereavement it is obviously a delicate
subject. The training session on bereavement is designed to
focus on two questions.

(a) What stage in the grief process has been reached, and

how can a visitor meet the bereaved in their pain and, if appropriate, help them to move on?

(b) How can a visitor help the bereaved person relate back to the church, where appropriate; and, in any case, how can the Christian faith of the visitor *serve* the bereaved person rather than exacerbate their pain?

Session 5 consists of role playing two bereavement visits, one before and one after the break. But it is also important that in this session the group begins to understand that its own responses to the ending of the course are relevant to learning. In a sense Sessions 5 and 6 (the final session) are both devoted to learning about this subject.

The visit by a church person to a bereaved family may well have features that set it apart from the visits of others. It is generally unexpected. It is occasioned by someone's care about the pain you are in. Experience suggests that bereaved people usually welcome such a visit. One aspect of this relates to the known faith of the visitor. They may be the first person on the scene who is perceived to be, so to speak, at home with death. This person, it is instinctively felt, has been here before. For the doctors death spelled failure, but here in a church visitor is someone who somehow has death included in their philosophy. Whatever your own relationship with Christian faith, at this moment anyhow, a Christian visitor can provide a welcome reference point in the midst of your howling pain and confusion. You do not expect them to conjure your grief away or explain it with ready answers. But at a time when you feel very vulnerable you may welcome the representative of a body you know has *something* to say about death.

The first part of the visit generally includes an account of the deceased person's illness and death, together with an account of the bereaved person's (or family's) feelings about that process. This will soon show if there is bitterness, anger or frustration accompanying the grief (for example, because of unsatisfactory treatment by the medical services) or whether, on the contrary, there is gratitude for kindnesses received, lack of suffering in death, or relief after a long illness. Grief is of course going on within these feelings, but to know them gives helpful leads to the visitor. There usually follows an account of the deceased person's relationship with the bereaved person, and this will probably move into an account of all their important relationships. It may well include a résumé of the person's life story, a showing of photographs, and an account of the consequences of the death for others involved in the bereavement. The bereaved person *may* go on to share other gnawing problems at quite a deep level. The visitor is not just passive in this process. There may be a need to offer a balance to strong emotions by tactfully enquiring about any feelings of gratitude, relief or (rarely) joy the bereaved person may have which thus far have been swamped by panic and pain. It may be that, without at all undermining the grieving process, the visitor can remind the bereaved person of their wider perspective. This should be done not so as to block or escape grieving but perhaps, on the contrary, to allow some additional emotion into the person's consciousness.

Experience suggests that such a visit can result in considerable *comfort* being brought to the bereaved person, which they can often be strangely surprised to feel. Where appropriate the visitor may find the opportunity to pray. If this proves possible it may be a powerful means of bringing relief, new hope, and of introducing a new sphere of experience which itself offers something to hold onto in this time of pain. Best of all, this new sphere cannot be taken away, and is not denied by the recent loss, whereas everything else *is* denied, spoiled, made valueless or meaningless to the senses, especially what you have long relied on to bring comfort and meaning, for many of these come from the person now taken from you. It is not, therefore, that the remembrance of God offers a last-ditch hope in an otherwise bleak time. More important, the remembrance of God in some mysterious way unites you to (rather than separates you from) your deeper instinctual security which is so much threatened by the rest of your bereaved feelings, and may even bring a sense of unity with your lost loved one. A good deal of the flavour of such a visit can be conveyed in a role play of a bereavement visit. It is soon shown to ruin things if the visitor rushes in with a too easy reassurance, a triumphalist conviction in resurrection or any attempt to avoid the pain of grief and let it be.

Session 6: Saying Goodbye and Evaluation

The final session begins with thinking about what sort of visits members of the group feel they might comfortably make. A review can be made of the sorts of situations which might come up in visiting. This leads into discussion of how a visitor might think of making an assessment of a visit. What, for example, *could* (and should) the church have taken on for that demanding old lady in Session 4? What is involved in making an assessment, and how do the visitors feel about doing it? The word assessment should not be understood too grandly. It is not leading up to a case conference. It simply refers to the comments the visitor will make on the bottom two inches of their referral form, and the question of either a subsequent visit or any further help the church (or other agency) might be able to give. Nevertheless it is an important aspect of the visit. A visitor needs to be clear as to how their visit has, or may have, contributed to helping someone and to be able to assess what else can or should be done.

The second half of the final session is devoted to an assessment of the course. Attention can be paid to saying goodbye at the end of a visit and saying goodbye to the course itself. The course assessment is done by looking again at the lists of expectations drawn up in Session 1 and comparing them with the course as experienced. This is an important chance for members of the group to speak frankly both about what they have enjoyed and what they feel critical about.

Saying Goodbye

A scheme needs to decide a policy on repeat visits. We set an initial maximum number of four. When a visitor knows they will go back again a date should be set. But visitors are advised not to let each visit continue for longer than an hour. Sometimes someone says something significant right at the end of a visit because they *don't* want to discuss it just yet. It does not mean the present visit should be extended. Saying goodbye is very important. Someone in need, especially if they are lonely, may feel sad and angry at the end of a visit. It is important for this to be acknowledged even if, as is probable, it is denied. In any case it is important not to avoid the saying of goodbye or the visit's value may be undermined. It can even be important to acknowledge what does not seem to have been too successful in the visit, as well as summing up what was good about it. It is also important not to expect people to be grateful, or to see that they have been helped. People can be helped to move on without realizing how it happened!

Practicalities

The visiting scheme in Tottenham followed a procedure which might easily be adapted to set up similar schemes in other UPA parishes:

1 Referrals for people (or families) to be visited come from the parish staff team. If church members wish to make a referral they do so by discussing it with a staff member;
2 The staff (in staff meeting) prepare a number of referral pro formas. The referral is cross-referenced with the parish files;
3 Completed forms go to the scheme co-ordinator, who matches them to visitors in the way that seems suitable. If there are more forms than visitors the scheme may not be able to cope. In this case the co-ordinator, having assessed priorities, returns outstanding forms to the staff;
4 The co-ordinator contacts the visitor and briefs them about their next visit;
5 The visitor makes the visit;
6 The visitor reports back to the co-ordinator. The referral form is completed and returned to the staff;
7 The staff consider what further pastoral action seems necessary;
8 The scheme pro forma is cross-referenced with the parish files and returned to the scheme's own file;
9 Visitors on the scheme meet once a month for a support group and to assess their experience.

[handwritten annotation] This is very sophisticated but it can be done elsewhere au like much A the book has nothing particularly LV. like UPA!

THIRTEEN

Conclusion: A Parish Profile

Teach us to care and not to care
Teach us to sit still.
                    T. S. Eliot.[1]

All Saints, Easterhope is a parish of 25,000 people set in a tough and troubled inner city area. It is a multi-ethnic parish with a large number of West Indians living in it. It contains the usual features of a UPA: bad housing, numbers of homeless and vagrant people, high unemployment, high crime rate, serious problems of drug and alcohol addiction, many elderly isolated people and a general lack of amenities.

The church is in the middle of the parish but divided from its housing estates by two main roads which leave it on an island. This is a snag since it makes it hard for the church to be a focus in the neighbourhood. On the other hand, since the parish is nearly a mile across, it prevents the church from being identified with one part of the parish rather than the other.

One member of the congregation of All Saints is called Bridget. Bridget is, at this moment, in church on a Sunday morning reflecting on her life over the last six years. The Eucharist has been prepared by the children who had spent yesterday together as part of a summer holiday programme. There is a team of ten who work with the children on a rota basis so that no one is too much excluded from worshipping with the adults. Bridget is in charge of this team. She is thirty-one and has three children of her own. She holds a part-time job serving behind the counter at Boots. She has no formal qualifications having left school at fifteen with no exam passes. Six years ago, Bridget thought, she would not have believed she would be running the children's programme of her local church. She had never been in it! One evening playing darts in the pub she had talked with a friend who went to church. Why? She didn't really know. She said the only way to find out was to come too. So Bridget had gone and been amazed. It was not as she had imagined. It was more fun but more serious. It seemed that something was going on which really mattered to these people.

Three things especially impressed her. First, the whole atmosphere. It was lively and joyful without being smug and hearty. In fact it was quite like the atmosphere in her regular pub. Then, secondly, Bridget was struck by the warmth of the welcome she was given at 'the Peace' though she was rather shocked by the blast of music from the speakers which seemed to belong more to a night club. She was even more impressed by watching the rest of the congregation. At 'the Peace' the service seemed to grind to a halt as people crossed from one part of the church to another to hug, laugh and exchange greetings. Everyone wanted to hug one woman in particular who it appeared had recently been bereaved. But the exchanges of greeting were all quite natural, spontaneous as in her own family at Christmas. There was nothing contrived about the atmosphere, which Bridget found delightful.

The third thing to impress her was everyone's *involvement*. The service wasn't as she imagined it would be—with the Vicar at the front and everyone quietly listening. In fact during the notices, to which about seven people contributed, someone shouted out, 'cobblers', but no one reacted, and in a later notice everyone clapped when a group called 'Amnesty' announced they'd helped get someone out of prison—it was all very odd. At the prayers many people contributed. Sarah, the friend from the pub, even prayed for her! But again there was nothing 'holy' and 'off-putting' about it; Sarah just said, 'Heavenly Father, be with Bridget and her family. May Bridget find a welcome in this church and her visit here be a blessing.' Everyone said 'Amen' and for some reason Bridget wanted to cry. She couldn't remember being so moved, though she couldn't have told you why. As for her children, they'd been swept off in the first hymn and when they came back later they were really excited about what they'd been doing (making puppets for a show the children were soon to put on) and they wanted to come back next week. At the communion they found themselves going up for a blessing, Bridget too. A woman put her hands on all their heads, gave them a rich smile and said a prayer. Again it was moving, and beyond words. The music and singing were lively and varied. They sang an old hymn Bridget remembered from school, but they also had new music, some of it accompanied not with the organ but by various people on all kinds of instruments. And there were several rounds though Bridget couldn't really follow the tune. It all seemed unusually *free*. Yet towards the end there was suddenly quite a long silence, except for the screeching of infants and the roar of traffic outside. The silence felt full of peace.

After church there was coffee and again she was made welcome. She bought a colourful straw basket and some tea from a stall selling products of the Third World. And she was disappointed when a man said, 'Are you new? oh good. Would you mind helping with . . .?', and someone else cut in, 'for heaven's sake leave her alone, Carlos, she's hardly walked in through the door.' Then she turned to Bridget and said with a grin, 'Forgive my enthusiastic friend here. He'll have your last ounce if you let him.' So she never found out what Carlos wanted her to do.

That was Bridget's introduction to All Saints. A group of elderly people sitting round in a ring had treated her as if they'd known her all their lives. She couldn't think when she'd met such people at once so friendly (though she was quite shocked by the way so much humour came out of such rude remarks) and yet so purposeful. For the church life seemed to be teeming with events and schemes and campaigns. She couldn't begin to sort it all out. And now, six years later, she was running the children's programme. One thing had led to another. First she'd joined an adult confirmation group leading after a year of house meetings to a retreat and confirmation. That was one milestone. Then the woman deacon suggested she might do an extension study course at a theological college in the Midlands. By post. And with a summer school. It took six months for her to decide to say yes. But she'd enjoyed it from the beginning and had even written some essays! After she started working with the children several people in the church had told her that she was 'a natural', though she had found this hard to believe, particularly when the Vicar had said, 'If I were the Bishop I'd ordain you like a shot.' True old Miss Hawkins couldn't have been bitchier. But then she always was to anyone who took the limelight away from her and her blessed vestry. And it couldn't be denied that Bridget had really discovered herself in this work with the children. She loved it.

She also knew she could never have done it without sustained encouragement. At one point she'd become depressed and wanted to give up the course. In fact she managed to work through as a result of the help she received from the deacon. This was something else she liked about All Saints. Though she gave a good deal to it she never felt taken for granted. Once at a diocesan meeting she'd met a church treasurer who said that at his parish the vicar was so involved with the finance he never met the person behind the treasurer; he might as well have been a computer. This contrasted with her experience of All Saints where she felt she mattered more as a person than as a functionary. And there was something else she liked about All Saints. Just when she and everyone else in the team were running out of ideas for the children's programme something would happen. There was a mixture of coherence and spontaneity in the church planning. A parish carnival, an event with a linked parish, something for presentation in church, a local community project, an exhibition — something would be on the calendar towards which the children could contribute. Sometimes it was Bridget and her team who had the ideas. Once they'd been the driving force behind a parish holiday for eighty, including a dozen elderly people. Another time they'd suggested an 'international day' with food from many countries which had been open to the public. 450 people had come and £1600 raised towards the 'Parish Café' project for addicts. But perhaps the most surprising thing was Bridget's learning to preach. Mostly this was as an interpreter or narrator for presentations made in church by the children, made, by the way, as a serious contribution to the worship, not as a sentimental showpiece ('aren't they sweet?') for everyone to applaud. But recently the vicar had asked her to preach in her own right. She'd protested but he'd been very persuasive — something about it being just what the church needed—the Worship Committee's idea so she couldn't blame him—and it would be fine provided the Bishop didn't turn up or he might want to close the church. Which he later explained was a joke. 'But true all the same.'

Araminta has been a churchwarden at All Saints since the last AGM. She is a single parent with two children aged eight and ten. Her mother lives nearby so she has always had plenty of help with the children. Until two years ago Araminta worked as a cleaner in a local factory. When this shut down she settled for the shorter hours of a school dinner lady; although this was less money it meant she could be at home when the children came back from school. Her mother had been a regular member of All Saints since 1959 but had always kept in the background. As a black woman she had never forgotten the three years of cold looks she'd had before people had slowly begun to be friendly. But Araminta had gone to church only occasionally, under some pressure, mostly for the sake of the children.

Then, two years ago, Araminta found herself at the centre of a major row. The church hall had been double-booked on a Saturday night. Araminta had organized a party to welcome a visiting Barbadian priest, an old friend of her mother's known to several West Indians in the parish. Most people invited were black. Unfortunately Eric and Sandra, both white (Sandra was a hairdresser and Eric, her boyfriend, hadn't found a job since leaving school two years ago) had arranged a 'Sixties Night' that Saturday for anyone in the church. In fact not many of Eric and Sandra's friends turned up. But the evening began with a forceful argument. Eric and Araminta had arrived at roughly the same time to set up in the hall. Instead of realizing, as they both should, that the fault lay with the hall secretary, they began to argue about what to do. Eric thought Araminta should have the party at her flat since they didn't need a space for dancing. Araminta said she'd booked the hall four months ago, long before Eric, and she needed it since it was possible that a large number might come. Eric said, 'That's the trouble with West Indians; you can't organize a party without half the neighbourhood coming—and I suppose you'll leave the usual mess. Last time there was a black party in the hall it took a month to clean up.' Araminta was angry. She flew at Eric, 'You're all the same; scratch any of you and there's a racist pushing to get out. You'd rather we all buggered off—back to the jungle I suppose. Well, I'll tell you something, Eric,' she raged, 'don't expect to see me or any black people at your smelly church ever again. I'll make sure of that!' and she stormed off leaving Eric and Sandra to their not very successful party. As the evening wore on Eric began to feel bad about what he'd said. Sandra had been furious with him. She thought that if Araminta had booked the hall first she definitely ought to have had it. Eric bravely decided to go round to Araminta's and apologize.

Araminta's party had been quite an airing of grievances about All Saints and its attitude to black people. This had only happened because Araminta had come home so upset. Months went by without such complaining, years in the case of some people. But Araminta's distress was too much. It triggered the feelings of the others who agreed that black and white didn't really meet at church. It was like a polite charade. Black people were very welcome provided they kept to the sidelines. So when Eric appeared there was, it must be admitted, a stony silence. Araminta started, a bit sharply, 'It's a bit late to give us the hall now, if that's why you've come.' Eric kept his peace. He apologized. He was obviously embarrassed. Apologizing was not Eric's strong point. In fact Araminta was genuinely touched by his apology; so were others. Araminta said, 'Well come in, meet our Father William and have a drink.' Eric stayed till 2 a.m. One or two people spoke simply but frankly to him about what it was like being black at All Saints. He had a long talk with Araminta. And it was this talk which sparked off in her the resolution that what she'd said outside the church hall was wrong. It was no good separating off. She'd try the opposite. She'd go to the vicar to see how West Indians could get more involved.

She did, and it was an important moment in the life of All Saints. The vicar had been deeply worried by the *suspicion* that the black people felt as Araminta described. Araminta's visit mobilized him. He preached about the split between black and white. He started to encourage black people particularly to take on responsibilities. He appealed to Araminta to stay with this problem, to do what she could to heal wounds, and be frank about what she saw. He asked if she would consider standing for the PCC, and the following year she was elected churchwarden. She is aware of the danger she might dominate the West Indians in the congregation, an awareness which helps her to encourage the others instead. This year, with Araminta as churchwarden, six other black members of the congregation have been voted onto the PCC. And there is general agreement that black and white are now a real community and that the church is much happier as a result.

Stan is the co-ordinator of the parish visiting scheme. His life has not been without problems. Some years ago he served a prison sentence for shoplifting, and before that he had been on drugs for a long time. After coming out of prison he found a job as a hospital porter and this had helped to settle him down. He eventually married a nurse and they now have a baby to whom Stan is entirely devoted. Stan started to come to church as a result of attending the local ecumenical marriage preparation course. Three years ago, soon after his marriage, he decided, after some coaxing by the woman deacon, to train as a pastoral visitor. The training was a revelation to Stan. He found he had a real talent for getting alongside people. The two leaders said they'd never seen anything like his ability in a role play which involved his visiting a depressed woman with an alcoholic and violent husband. Eighteen months later Stan was leading one of the support groups for visitors on the scheme. And recently he had taken over-all charge of its ninety volunteers.

Stan's main hang-up is a sense of inferiority about his understanding of religion. He enjoys the services but reckons he doesn't understand a word of what is being said. He claims he can't make head or tail of sermons and is constantly telling the clergy to talk so that, 'The likes of people like me can see what yer' on abaht.' For months Stan tried going to a weekly house group aimed at exploring the faith. But it made him more confused, and he even started to get bored and depressed, feeling unable to take part. A breakthrough came when a nineteen-year-old art student offered to run a Lent Group on Saturday mornings to look at the meaning of Christianity using what she called 'colours, feelings and objects'. In this group, after meditation (which Stan had

grown to appreciate), instead of *talking* about belief, a
Christian symbol, such as resurrection, was taken as a focus.
After a time of reflection and sharing, the group *made*
something, using colours, wire, paper, cardboard and sellotape,
to express its meaning for them. Here at last was an approach
Stan felt at home with. And he has started a part time course
in art and design at the Technical College as a result.

The other main strand in Stan's church involvement is
political. He feels passionately that not enough is done for ex-
offenders and that British prisons are in need of reform, so
he's a keen member of one of the church's liveliest groups
called 'Action for Justice' and is always encouraging them to
do something about prisons. So far they have written to the
MP and the Home Secretary to protest at overcrowding and
prison conditions. They have organized a community petition
(called 'Ten improvements to prisons needed now') and they
have had the Chaplain General of the prisons giving a public
talk in the local town hall. This may not seem much, but in
fact the main thrust of the 'Action for Justice' group is
directed elsewhere: towards a local co-operative housing trust,
a drop-in café, and a link with a church in Namibia.

The difficulty with sketching a profile of All Saints is that
it contains such a wide variety of people. There are several
teachers, various community workers, two doctors, quite a
lot of students, home helps, cleaners, unemployed people,
senior citizens, disabled people, a policeman, a traffic warden,
various civil servants, housewives, nurses, health visitors,
labourers, bus conductors, postal workers, telephonists,
secretaries, caretakers, a photographer, a psychotherapist
and a dental assistant. There are single parents, gays,
children, teenagers, West Indians, Asians, Africans, Chinese,
and Spanish. There are ex-Catholics, ex-Methodists, ex-
Baptists, agnostics and one couple who come regularly but
claim to be 'Zen Buddhist really'. It is an allegiance to All
Saints which somehow holds all this together. And though a
trained theologian could appreciate the almost conservative
Anglicanism lying at the heart of the worship and what is
preached and practised at All Saints, very few of its members
would (if one is being honest) pass a simple test in the
rudiments of Anglican orthodoxy. What is not in doubt is
how much their belonging means to them. The particular

attraction differs. It may be the church's worship, its social life, its concern to understand Christian faith in the modern world, its openness, its ecumenical spirit, the warmth of its fellowship, its local and political commitment, its varied approach (like the art student's Saturday group, the gardening group or the music group), or its pastoral outreach. Whatever the emphasis for each individual most members well appreciate that its primary reason for being is to seek after God, to love and worship God, and to attempt to put the Second Commandment into practice in an organized way. There would be general agreement that the important thing at All Saints is to come as you are and discover the mystery of God in your own way. There would be general prejudice against any idea of Christianity that tried to prepackage God in right doctrine, correct formulae and a party line so that you had to adjust your personality and experience to fit this before feeling at home in All Saints. All Saints, it might be said, is for people first, and to encourage Christians second.

But even the briefest introduction to All Saints would be incomplete without meeting the Vicar, *Brian Adams*. Brian is married, thirty-six, conscientious, attractive, humorous and a dreadful worrier. He has been in the parish for four years and feels his work has only just begun. The Bishop is concerned that he might make himself ill or damage his family life (no children as yet and a wife who's a doctor) and Brian tries to limit his work to a thirteen-hour day, with one and a half days off a week. He doesn't always succeed.

Brian is clear that his priorities so far have been to engender a supple and open feel in the congregation, a much deeper sense of community between black and white members, lively worship, integration of the church's diverse activities to make them a coherent operation, a more pervasive spirit of prayer, better links with local agencies (especially schools) and a response to unemployment. This last, and one personal anguish combine to keep him awake at night.

The personal anguish is that after four years Brian, though a self-adjusted person, is no further forward in protecting his own vulnerability when personally attacked. In the last few months Miss Hawkins has been constantly sour, always comparing Brian unfavourably with the previous vicar and criticizing every aspect of life at All Saints. Many times Brian

has nearly lost his temper and blurted out, as a streak of him
so ardently wishes to do, 'Well if that's how you feel why
don't you bloody well leave.' But then Miss Hawkins is the
longest-serving member at All Saints and some of the
deficiencies so piercingly articulated by her are all too
apparent. Criticism and apparent rejection such as this hurts
Brian deeply. Last Sunday for example, a family walked out
after the Peace because, he later discovered, he had 'deliberately
spurned' them by greeting people on the next row rather than
them. An elderly lady, visited regularly through the pastoral
visiting scheme and by Brian once a month, had said to him,
'You don't give a damn about anything except getting your
picture in the Easterhope Gazette.' Even his own clergy
colleagues can be vicious; or at least that's how he took it
when another vicar from the deanery asked him whether All
Saints had joined the Liberal Atheists yet, 'or are you still
pretending to be Christians?'.

His pain is Brian's secret. Everyone except his wife knows
Brian as extrovert, confident, full of zest, resilience and *joie
de vivre*. They are right. What they don't see are the wounds
he carries from continually absorbing the sad destructiveness
of those too internally scarred to contain their own pain.
Brian's other major worry is the church's failure to do
something about unemployment. On account of restoration
debts, the church is in the process of raising £90,000 for
repairs to the church fabric. Money is therefore worryingly
short despite a well organized stewardship programme. There
is no church plant which could be further exploited for work
with the unemployed. Yet Brian knows that other inner city
churches operate impressive employment schemes using
government or sponsorship funds. Alas so far All Saints has
come up with nothing specific for the unemployed. Next
week he has arranged for some local borough officers, a ward
councillor and two members of the nearby Industrial Mission
team to attend the local ecumenical clergy fraternal to see if
there are initiatives which the churches might be able to
develop.

All Saints, then, faces an unanswered question: is it to
hope that some further project comes out of the meeting?
Faith in the City suggests that it might. And surely something
for the unemployed would be helpful and is desperately

needed. But perhaps All Saints already has a full load. It is a community of 200 members. It has activities and commitments galore. It is a worshipping, learning, healing and serving community. Perhaps Brian and the congregation must learn where to stop. God's Kingdom can only be glimpsed in Easterhope and All Saints is not called to build heaven on earth. Brian has yet to accept the excruciating necessity of inner city ministry, that is to accept the vast imbalance between what is required and what it is possible to achieve. Brian and All Saints must continue learning to live in the tension of knowing how great is the need and somehow, at least sometimes, going to their prayers in peace.

Notes

1. T. S. Eliot, 'Ash Wednesday' in *Collected Poems 1909—1962*, Faber and Faber 1963.

Index